Bible
Study
for
Busy
Women

Bible
Study
for
Busy
Women

ETHEL L. HERR

MOODY PRESS
CHICAGO

©1983 by
ETHEL L. HERR

Library of Congress Cataloging in Publication Data

Herr, Ethel L.
  Bible study for busy women.

  Includes bibliographical references.
  1. Bible—Study. 2. Women—Religious life. I. Title.
BS600.2.H45 1982b   220'.07   82-20890
ISBN 0-8024-0417-3

2 3 4 5 Printing/EB/Year 87 86 85 84 83

To my ladies' class at Valley Church—
patient, receptive,
hard-working
students of the Bible
and treasured sisters and friends

Contents

Acknowledgments

Just before I entered my teens, three apparently insignificant things happened to me. But they changed the direction of my life.

First, I signed a pledge card for a youth organization in which I was never active. One of the items on that card read, "I will read my Bible every day." It was a novel idea to me, but I had promised, so I began at least to try.

Second, the Lord gave me a Sunday school teacher who did more than read her teacher's manual as she prepared her lessons. Each week she brought us exciting tidbits of information and challenge that she had gleaned from some Bible study books. I do not remember any of the facts she shared, but I will never forget the impression her diligence made on me—Bible study was exciting!

Finally, a neighbor gave our family several books from a deceased minister's library. Among them was a yellowed volume with a simple title like "How to Study the Bible." I devoured it. That was the beginning of a life-long adventure with Bible study.

As I begin to list all the people who made a measurable contribution to this book, I must start with the elderly schoolteacher who gave me the pledge card to sign, the housewife Sunday school teacher who modeled excitement, and the neighbor who unloaded his discarded books onto our shelves. My list goes on to include youth leaders, personal friends, college professors from Multnomah School of the Bible, pastors, Sunday school teachers, and neighborhood classes of women and children I have taught for the past thirty years.

Most recently, I am grateful to my pastor, Paul Steele, who invited me to teach a class on Bible study methods to the women of Valley Church in Cupertino, California; to Leland Ryken for his book *The Literature of the Bible,* which opened some exciting new doors and stimulated my mind and heart as I rethought all I had learned and found a shape for the series of lessons; to each lady who stayed with me in that class for nine months of weekly sessions; to Les Stobbe, now of Here's Life Publishers, for his confidence that urged me to cut the course down to size and share it on paper; to my writing critique group who listened and advised me through the final stages of manuscript preparation; and to my dear mother, who, as always, eagerly proofread the manuscript.

Above all, I offer my inexpressible gratitude to God Himself for giving to us all His Bible, a Book well worth getting excited about and giving our lives to.

Introduction

Nancy loved her weekly Bible study class at the church downtown. Lectures opened up to her undreamed-of vistas of truth. Discussion groups allowed her to share exciting discoveries she made as she answered questions during the week. She reveled in the joy of forming new friendships and learning from the small group. For several years those interchurch studies had been a major source of spiritual nourishment for her Christian life.

When the class ended last spring, though, Nancy faced a dilemma. She had completed the cycle covered by the classes. No more were available. What would she do next? Could she find another teacher who could lead her as well? Who could help her find in the Bible the direction she needed for handling her specific problems?

She tried to find a solution. No new teachers presented themselves. She found many study guidebooks in the bookstore, but none quite seemed to speak to her needs at the moment.

"You can learn to study the Bible for yourself," her pastor's wife assured her.

"But I need a plan to work by," she insisted. "I am much too undisciplined to handle it without some guidance."

Many women today feel a lot like Nancy. They recognize the value of personal, individualized Bible study, but are unable to plan it themselves or find a prepared plan that fits them. Even the books on Bible study methods they find are often vague and unspecific or too technical and scholarly to help them bring God's messages down to the soapsuds and unmade beds where they live.

So they either settle for a study that is not on target or make a dozen false starts at some sort of study that never offers them more than a surface treatment of subjects that require in-depth coverage. Worse yet, many finally give up altogether and content themselves with Sunday-morning-from-the-pulpit rations and random sampling readings over morning cups of coffee.

Bible Study for Busy Women was written to assure Nancy and the thousands like her that you can learn to study the Bible for yourself. In the pages that follow, I will attempt to give you the know-how to make your dream become a reality.

Bible study will never be a matter of mastering one simple formula. No one can give you ten easy steps to full Bible knowledge. And though there are some basic principles, the application of those principles in methods varies. That is true in part because our Bible comes from a God of creative diversity. He rarely acts according to predictable, routine patterns. He has planned His Book so that it contains a unique combination of different types of literature—history, philosophy, poetry, law, romance, personal letters, adventure, sermons, and many others. We simply cannot expect to study everything in such a varied Book by using a single method. The nature of the Bible demands that we use a broad spectrum of study approaches if we are to grasp its meanings and apply it to our lives.

In general, study methods fall into three categories: First, *panoramic methods*. When you take your camera to the crest of a hill and photograph the scene spread out for miles before you, you get a panoramic view. Some Bible studies are like that. Single-sitting readings of a Bible book, read-the-Bible-through-in-a-year plans, broad topical studies—those are panoramic studies.

Second, *zoom lens methods*. As you stand on the same hilltop and attach a zoom lens to your camera, you can focus in on one small clump of trees several hundred feet distant, and bring them close enough for careful scrutiny. Many Bible studies do that—book studies, limited topical studies, character studies, chapter studies, and others.

Third, *microscopic methods.* When you walk down off the hill to one tree in your chosen clump, you may pick a single leaf and examine it under a microscope. That is like the slower, detailed types of study—verse studies, word studies, studies of prayers, poetry, parables, and the like.

We need to become familiar with all those approaches. If we never see the panoramic view, we cannot understand how the microscopic pieces fit together, and may misconstrue the things we see. On the other hand, the zoom lens and microscopic realms are where we breathe and make daily decisions. So, of what value is the panorama without the zoom lens or microscopic view?

We need various types of study methods to insure for ourselves daily fresh learning experiences. When we always do things the same way, we fall easily into the proverbial rut that is so ungodlike. Down in this rut, we miss a whole world of fresh newness. We lose our keen ability to look for new ideas and observe and do new things.

As we grow in all areas of life, our need for God's truth and our capacities to appreciate and assimilate it change. An approach that helps us tremendously today may not do anything for us tomorrow. At times, we need to study comforting passages of Scripture so the Lord can minister healing to our bruised spirits. At other times, we need to study the prayers of the Bible to learn how to pray and accept God's answers. Sometimes we need to research a specific problem or trace God's dealings with people in a biographical study. How or what we study often depends on our needs at the moment.

Finally, our personalities have something to do with the type of study that speaks to us. An engineer thrives on analytical studies. He prepares charts, studies detailed relationships of words to each other, learns Hebrew and Greek, and dissects the Scriptures in a hundred ways. A homemaker usually is not as excited about such details and may get hopelessly lost in diagrams and charts. She will probably profit much more from a study of how God worked in the life of some woman in the Bible or what He has to say in the epistles about practical everyday living. If you are an artist, you will enjoy a study of art in the Bible. Teachers and counselors learn from Jesus' teaching and counseling techniques. What methods of study you can best use often depends on who you are, where you are coming from, and what your personality is.

As you approach some of the studies in this book, you may not feel you can handle them. That will be a normal reaction. Give them a try anyway. You may be surprised at how well some of them fit you. Further, some that you cannot handle today may be just what you need tomorrow. If you have exposed yourself to them now, when you are ready for them you will have all the materials available and know how to go about it.

This book is designed to help you get started and to give you the tools for a lifetime of exciting personal Bible study discoveries. You may study it alone or in a group, with or without a teacher. Set your own pace, but do push on to completion.

J. I Packer, in his introduction to the book *Knowing Scripture* by R. C. Sproul, makes a clear and clever case for the importance of Bible study when he says:

> If I were the devil. . . , one of my first aims would be to stop folk from digging into the Bible. Knowing that it is the Word of God, teaching men to know and love and serve the God of the Word, I should do all I could to surround it with the spiritual equivalent of pits, thorn hedges and man traps, to frighten people off.[1]

If we want to learn to study the Bible for ourselves, we must determine that Satan will not succeed in accomplishing his evil purpose of keeping us from all the invaluable riches God's Word holds for the diligent seeker.

---

1. J. I. Packer, in R. C. Sproul, *Knowing Scripture* (Downer's Grove, Ill.: Inter-Varsity, 1977), pp. 9-10.

LESSON 1

Getting Ready
to Study the Bible

The woman who studies her Bible every day and allows God to fashion her life by its patterns enjoys certain privileges not available to her in any other way.

She receives regular, personal messages from the Creator of the universe.

She learns what God is like and what He is doing on this earth.

She learns the answers to many difficult questions of science, history, psychology, and the future.

She knows who she is, why she is here, and how to maintain a warm relationship with God.

She has a purpose for living and some dependable criteria for setting priorities.

She experiences assurance, comfort, guidance, strength, and freedom from guilt.

She has infinite resources for helping others in need.

She has every reason to face life's calamities and mysteries with an unpanicky confidence in the God who knows and understands all things.

She has the immense satisfaction of knowing that she is bringing pleasure to the heart of God.

If being an obedient Bible student does all that for women in today's pressurized homes, neighborhoods, and career circles, why is it that so few women become Bible students?

Women (and men as well) who may see the value of regular Bible study offer many excuses for not doing it. Most of their ideas can be summarized in the following four statements.

First, *"It is too difficult to understand the Bible!"* Who has not felt this way at times, while reading some obscure passage? The Bible does indeed offer many things that are far beyond the understanding of the novice student. Even mature students have difficulties with parts of this divine textbook.

However, just because we cannot understand it all is not a valid reason for not studying the things we can handle. We will never come to understand anything if we do not try. The Bible presents many levels of spiritual truth—milk for newborn babies in the Christian life, vegetables for growing youngsters, and meat and strong food for mature adults. Part of the unique genius of Scripture is the fact that it contains something for every level of human growth.

It only makes sense that if the God of the universe took time and effort to reveal Himself in His Word, He surely did it in such a way that we could understand those things we are ready to learn and use. It has been said that the "Bible was written to ordinary people involved in the dailiness of living." The Bible makes this claim for its relevancy:

> All scripture is inspired by God and is useful for teaching the faith and correcting error, for resetting the direction of a man's life and training him in good living. The scriptures are the comprehensive equipment of the man of God, and fit him fully for all branches of his work. [2 Timothy 3:16, Phillips*]

The first key to understanding the Bible lies in being diligent to search out and apply those portions that match our spiritual maturity level and cause us to stretch and grow. When we do that, it is not too difficult to understand.

A second reason some people offer for not studying their Bibles is, *"It's too boring!"* When I hear that excuse, I suspect

New Testament in Modern English.

that one of three things is true about the person. Either (1) she does not know Jesus Christ personally and has no basis for spiritual recognition or understanding, (2) she has not read her Bible for so long that she has lost her appetite for it, or (3) she has allowed some sin or busyness to cool her love for Jesus Christ and is hence no longer interested in what He has to say to her.

A friend for whom I had prayed a long time once told me, "A year ago, I thought most of the Bible was dead and boring. Now, since I have come to know the Lord personally and have developed a hunger for His truth, I cannot read enough. Why did I waste so many years getting started?"

I have gone through periods in my life when the Bible seemed dry and cold. While I was in the hospital with my third baby, the night nurse, a Christian, shared with me her testimony. "I have been a Christian for many years," she told me. "But I can honestly say that every time I open my Bible, I still get excited about what I read there."

I nodded and mumbled some sort of agreement with her sentiment. But after she left, reflecting on her enthusiasm, I had to admit to myself that it had been a long time since I could say what she had said tonight and mean it. I had been studying my Bible since I was a teenager. Never before had it occurred to me that somewhere along the line, I had lost the excitement—my Bible had become dry, even boring at times.

That night, a yearning to restore the enthusiasm was born in my heart. Gradually, over the next year, as the Lord dealt with some problems of self-sufficiency and misdirected priorities, I began once again to recapture a genuine hunger for God's Word so that it came alive.

A third excuse for not studying the Bible is, *"It's too much work!"* That excuse is absolutely true, unless our spirits are genuinely hungry. Bible study is work. We cannot hastily read a daily verse, morning and evening, then go on our ways and expect by some sort of supernatural magic that the Bible will seep into us and change our lives. We do not have to be told that we learn to cook by cooking, to sew by sewing, to play

tennis by playing tennis. Bible study works by the same principle. We will never learn to study the Bible simply by reading
books that tell us how to do it. For that reason, in this book we
have included an assignment in Bible study with each lesson.
If you barge on past the assignments without doing them and
sail through all the chapters like some mad tourist attempting
to hit all the highlights of Europe in two weeks, you will never learn to study your Bible.

If, on the other hand, you are hungry to know what God
has to say to you today, tomorrow, and every day, you will never consider it too much work.

I once read of a young man who approached an elderly Bible teacher and asked, "How can I gain all the knowledge of
the Bible you have?"

The older man answered without hesitation: "It is very
simple. Just study it every day for the next fifty years."

A final reason offered by non-students is this: *"I don't know
how."* By the time you have completed this book and its assignments, you can never again use that excuse.

Once our excuses are eliminated we are not yet ready to
study in earnest. It is possible to learn the Word of God and
gain a thorough head knowledge but never live by its pre-
cepts. I have known people like that. They know all the answers, the facts, the who-did-what-and-when-and-where-and-
why's. But their lives are cold, sterile, unfruitful in terms of
spiritual realities.

As we approach the Bible, we need to develop four right attitudes so that what we learn will affect the way we live. First,
we need an open heart and mind. Each of us is born with a
sinful, anti-God nature. We naturally possess a wisdom that is
based on mere human reasoning. Only when the Spirit of God
lives in us do we have the resources to see things from God's
point of view. Without those resources, we can never expect to
understand God's Book and His truth (see 1 Corinthians
2:14).

Opening our hearts and minds begins, then, when we recognize our spiritual and moral bankruptcy (Romans 3:23) and

receive Jesus Christ personally as our Savior and Lord (John 1:12-13). At that point, He sends His Spirit to be our Companion, Interpreter, and Teacher of His words (see John 3:5; 14:26; 1 Corinthians 3:16; Ephesians 1:12-13).

Openness goes on, however, to involve maintaining a humble, teachable spirit. That is one of the first things the enemy of our souls will snatch from us, if we are not vigilant. Finally, having an open heart means being expectant and excited, believing that God is going to teach us through the power of His Holy Spirit because He delights to do so. We need to pray, as did the psalmist, "Open my eyes that I may behold wonderful things from Thy law" (Psalm 119:18).

A second attitude necessary for effective Bible study is a genuine hunger for knowledge and spiritual food. We have already noted that if we are not hungry, Bible study becomes a chore. First Peter 2:2 tells us to desire the milk of the Word in the same way that a baby hungers for food. Doctors claim that a baby cries when he is hungry because he feels literal hunger pains. God expects us to crave spiritual food with the same intensity of a baby needing food, to have a desire so strong that we are in pain until we can be fed.

I once had a Bible teacher like that. Following his conversion, as a young man, he experienced such strong spiritual hunger pains that he would come home from a long day at work and directly start reading his Bible. Often he read nonstop into the night—sometimes even until morning. Today, he has major portions of Scripture memorized and teaches with a unique reverence for and acquaintance with this special Book.

Third, Bible study will never even happen unless we give it a top priority on our busy schedules. I have seen books that claim to give readers simple Bible study methods for short periods of time. Do this study in five minutes, this one in ten, and the other in half an hour. Such promises are misleading. We simply cannot fit something as demanding as effective Bible study into the scrappy chinks of spare time chiseled out of overcrowded schedules. The only way a busy person can find time to study her Bible is to *make* it. We have to say that it is number one in importance, then arrange the rest of our lives accordingly.

Such priority scheduling calls for some common sense and flexibility. When my family comes home expecting dinner, I cannot in all good conscience tell them, "Sorry about dinner tonight. Too many emergencies got in the way of my Bible study today. So I have to spend my time in the Word rather than in the kitchen."

Giving Bible study a top priority means juggling relationships and responsibilities around and lopping off some of the unnecessary things to make room for what is most important. At times, it even means missing a study session for a true emergency situation. We must take special care never to give our growing families the impression that Bible study is more important than they are and that it therefore has the right to impinge on family needs. The godly woman, living daily by God's Word, will find creative ways to meet family obligations and still schedule time to dig into her Bible.

Finally, we need to recognize the difference between Bible reading and Bible study and consistently practice both.

Bible *reading* gives us an overview, a general impression, some panoramic facts and quick ideas. As I read my Bible, I am walking down a pathway and picking up loose treasures that lie scattered on the surface of the ground.

Bible *study* is another story. Here, I dig beneath the surface and find the hidden treasures along the pathway. There is a lot more underneath than on the top. Digging to study often involves searching out the situations, the conditions of the person who was experiencing the thing I read about in my Bible.

For instance, I may read how Abram left Ur of the Chaldees and followed God's leading to a wild new land called Canaan. In a cursory reading, I will learn many facts and get an interesting glimpse of the man who became the father of the Hebrew people. I may even glean a few lessons in obedience, consistency, and human relations.

If, in addition to that, I study my atlas and encyclopedia to learn where Ur was, what it was like, who Abram was, and what he was leaving behind, I have a basis for understanding that God was asking him to make the ultimate sacrifice of his day. Then I can translate that into terms of what God asks of me today. I realize that when He speaks, He may ask me, too, to make the ultimate sacrifice for Him—not to leave a heathen city and settle in some unknown wasteland, but perhaps to give up some ungodly friendship or to change jobs, or to serve an unlovely, demanding person. If I have no idea who Abram was, how wealthy he was, how much he left behind, how desolate the land was to which God led him, how little he knew of God and His ways, then Abram's story will have little meaning to me.

At the outset of our studies together, I think we can summarize our expectations of the Bible study process by listing ten simple rules to guide us.

1. Be consistent. Spend some time every day. We do not gorge our stomachs at the dinner table on Sunday and starve for the rest of the week because it is too much trouble to cook every day. If we did, we could neither digest nor appreciate our food. So it is with the Bible. If we think of God's Word as food vital for our soul's growth, we will have no trouble remembering that we have to study it daily to make it a part of us.

2. Be systematic. The purpose of these lessons is to give you a set of systematic approaches to Bible study. God does not speak to us as we waken each morning, yawn, open our Bibles and, bleary-eyed, read the first verse we see. Nor does He jump out at us from random spottings of isolated texts snatched between hurried appointments during the day. We need to make a plan and follow it.

3. Make notes of your Bible study. Keep a small notebook with your Bible, in which you record your thoughts as you study.

4. Ask questions. Some people think it is almost sacrilegious to ask questions of the Bible. The truth is that if we do

not ask questions, we learn very little. The question mark is sanctified. So never fear to use it.

5. Be prayerful. Ephesians 1:15-19 is a beautiful example of the kind of prayer we should pray before we read or study the Bible: "I pray that the eyes of your heart may be enlightened so that you may know what is the hope of His calling, what are the riches of the glory of His inheritance in the saints, and what is the surpassing greatness of His power toward us who believe" (vv. 18-19a).

We desperately need to pray for His enlightenment if our study is to reveal to us all God wants to teach us. He is, after all, our Teacher.

6. Be persistent and adaptable. It is easy to say, "Today I don't feel like studying, Lord, so I probably won't get much out of it." Do not believe that lie! Even when you do not feel as though you got a thing, you take away something, perhaps only in your subconscious. In a time of real need, down the line somewhere, the thing you learned in your dry hour will surface to give you strength.

Be patient with yourself and with God and stick with the effort. Do not be in a rush. If you learn only one thing a day, that is far more important than filling out a complete worksheet and not graspng any of it. We all have those times when God seems distant and no matter what we do, we cannot seem to break the pattern. If we give up in such times and settle for less than consistency, we will never give God the chance to break our non-learning pattern and fill us with His truth.

7. Be obedient. God does not reveal truth to curiosity seekers. Rather, He reveals it to sincere disciples whose primary goal in life is to please Him by doing everything He asks of them.

8. Share what you learn with someone else. You can gather a group of friends to share the things you learn in these and other studies. Or, if you remain open to God, He will give you opportunities to share with families, friends, even strangers in unexpected places.

9. Keep a record of ideas for future studies. As you study,

new ideas will arrest your attention and entice you to follow them down sideroads NOW. Resist the temptation and go on with what you are doing. But not before you have added those ideas to a special section of your notebook. When you finish the studies you are working on you will find the list helpful in giving you direction for the next venture. (At the end of this lesson, you will find a worksheet to use throughout this course as a place to list your new ideas.)

10. Never allow personal Bible study to take the place of Bible study groups or church attendance, where you are fed by your Christian brothers and sisters. God teaches us some things directly through our study and others through the special ministry of the servants whom He has gifted to teach us in His Body.

Two kinds of people take Bible study classes and read books on Bible study methods. These are what one Christian art teacher used to call *students* and *disciples*.[1] A *student* learns everything a teacher teaches him. A *disciple* goes beyond that; he takes the teacher's ideas and runs with them. As author of this book, I am looking primarily not for students, but for disciples—women who will take these studies, use them creatively, expand them, and run with them. I pray that you will do life-changing things with what you learn here. When you have finished these studies, you will be ready to share them with someone else. But you will add a dimension of depth and experience that is all your own, a dimension that comes from being a creative, productive disciple who learns with head and heart and dresses it all in practical shoe leather.

ASSIGNMENT

Read Genesis 1-4. As you read, record in your notebook the following things suggested by your reading:

1. Questions
2. New discoveries

---

1. Hans Rookmaker, Dutch art professor and founder of a Dutch L'Abri community. See Linette Martin, *Hans Rookmaker: A Biography* (Downer's Grove, Ill.: Inter-Varsity, 1979), p. 134.

3. Ideas about God
4. Ideas about man
5. Commands to obey
6. Promises to claim
7. Examples to follow or to avoid
8. Anything else that seems important to you

FUTURE IDEAS WORKSHEET

On this sheet, record any ideas that come to you for studies you would like to do in the future. Add to the list with each study you do through this book.

Devotional studies:

Paraphrases:

Stories:

Prayers:

Poetry:

Parables:

Biographies:

Problem-solving studies:

Others:

LESSON 2

What Is
the Bible?

What is the Bible?

If you were to ask that question of five of your neighbors, you would probably receive five different answers, such as:

"A great book for inspiring noble character."

"The official textbook of Christianity."

"A quaint collection of ancient myths and impossible-to-live-by goody-goody sermons."

"A work of fine literature."

"A special book that contains some divine words."

Although nearly every family on your block owns a copy of the Bible, most of them are quite ignorant of its content and message. Many may not even be able to locate it among their possessions. Only a few people in our society have ever allowed the Bible to arrest their serious attention.

You are among those few. You know that the Bible is no ordinary book. You come to it expecting something unique that no other book can provide. Are your expectations realistic? What makes this book special? What is it designed by God to do for you? What gives it the ability to meet your needs in the ordinariness and perplexities of being a woman in affluent, secular, space-age America?

The Bible is many things. First (and most obvious), *it is an amazing library of sixty-six volumes.* Lying side by side on its shelves, we find history, love stories, law codes, poetry, sermons, prophecies, genealogies, pithy proverbs, biographies, and parables. In a rich variety of style and form, God has given us a vivid picture of over 1600 years of His intervention in the affairs of men, along with His pattern for such intervention for the rest of human history and on into eternity.

Second, *the Bible is a work of philosophy and morals.* Many people who are unwilling to believe the Bible implicitly or commit themselves to the God of the Bible nevertheless recognize the value of its logical system of philosophical thought and its high standard of morals and ethics.

Third, *the Bible is a work of expert literary craftsmanship.* Teachers of English literature have long praised its excellence. Like all great literature, it is characterized by these four things:

1. It is based on concrete examples of people involved in common human experiences. It is not a series of vague, complex, or rambling philosophical essays that cannot be translated into action in everyday life. Rather, through the lives of real people facing real problems, it shows us how to live by God's patterns and the consequences of not doing so.

2. It presents those experiences in such a way that they illustrate God's viewpoint on human existence. Human experiences become His teaching tool to show us what God is like and what He expects of us. All great literature takes the raw materials of disorganized life and arranges them in a patterned order so as to give them meaning. The Bible does that masterfully, and then applies the principles thus learned to our daily lives.

3. It shares truth in artistic form. God, as Creator, is also the Author of art. Through the writing of His Book, He showed that the beauty of form used in presenting His truth was as important as its content. As such, it demanded special attention and care.

Among other things, that means that God used artistic lan-

guage to communicate difficult eternal concepts to our limited human minds. In Isaiah 55:8, God says: "For My thoughts
are not your thoughts, neither are your ways My ways." This
is a picture of God up in heaven longing to communicate
with us down on earth. Things that are normal in His experience are foreign to us. How is He going to explain Himself
so we can grasp His meaning? Verses 10 and 11 tell us how:

> For as the rain and the snow come down from heaven, and
> do not return there without watering the earth, and making
> it bear and sprout, and furnishing seed to the sower and
> bread to the eater; so shall My word be which goes forth
> from My mouth; it shall not return to Me empty, without
> accomplishing what I desire.

He accommodated Himself to our mentality and sphere of
experience by using word pictures that we could understand.
The form God used here is known as imagery—painting a
picture of something we know about (rain and crops) to teach
us about something He wants us to learn (the effectiveness of
His Word). Not only imagery, but most of the artistic forms in
Scripture are primarily accommodations to our limited human
understandings.

4. It has enduring quality. Time has a way of revealing
greatness in art of all sorts. The fact that the Bible has en-
dured so long as a respected work of literature says something
not only about God's power to protect what is His for our use;
it also serves as evidence of this Book's true literary greatness.

The Bible, then, is a library, a textbook of philosophy and
morals, and a literary masterpiece. Fourth, and most important, *it is God's personal message to His beloved human creatures.* Again, we recall that 2 Timothy 3:16 tells us that "all
Scripture is given by inspiration of God." Literally, it says it is
"God-breathed." The Bible is God's written verbal expression
of His heart, mind, and Person, and His laws and guidelines
for faith and daily living. As such, it is both totally adequate
for setting standards of belief and conduct and completely reliable. We can confidently believe every word to be the accurate, authoritative, and practical Word of our ultimately absolute God.

Inspiration had a human side as well. Second Peter 1:21 says, "Men moved [or carried along as a ship carries its passengers] by the Holy Spirit spoke from God."

The thing that truly amazes me is that although all of this book is God-breathed, it clearly reflects the personalities of the human individuals God used to write it. I never hope to understand how God could take over forty human writers—with different personalities, abilities, cultural backgrounds, and occupations, some literary and others uneducated—over a period of at least 1600 years, communicating in two major languages and several minor ones, and produce a marvelously unified, consistent book structured like a planned manuscript. My mind is so human-bound that if I try to comprehend the miracle of it, I only become confused. The most I can do is recognize it as the work of an infinitely powerful and creative God, who is terribly eager to reveal Himself to me.

Because the Bible is completely inspired by God, despite its variety of writers, styles, and forms, it has a striking unity of theme running from Genesis 1 through Revelation 22. The entire message of this complex book can be summarized in twenty-five words: The creation, distortion, and restoration of God's image in man. Restoration provided by the loving, sacrificial death and miraculous resurrection of God's incarnate Son, Jesus Christ.

The Bible can be likened to a graceful pearl necklace. Each pearl on the string is a separate entity, beautiful and valuable in its own right. Without the string, however, it ceases to be a necklace and falls into a disarrayed heap of jewels, difficult to use and appreciate. Some people see the Bible in that way, as a disconnected collection of choice gems, but with no overall significance or power to bring beauty and order into their lives. The best they can do with such a Bible is dip into its pages here and there and extract gems from the heap to admire and struggle to make a place for in their lives. When we know the central theme of the Bible, that theme becomes the string that holds all the nuggets of truth together, gives it impact, and changes and beautifies our lives.

We might also say the Bible has one giant plot. By plot, we do not mean a man-made, fictitious story line. The plot is the progressive development of a story. As with stories of all kinds, true or fictional, the Bible is plotted, as is evidenced by the following three elements.

1. Conflict. The Scriptures are based on the supreme conflict between God and Satan, good and evil, man's will and God's will. On every page, we see people in conflict with one another, with themselves, and with God. An important part of the conflict involves making choices between their ways of thinking and acting and God's ways. All of this is a part of the basic conflict between God and Satan for the mastery of the human race.

2. Progression toward a goal. The Bible is a masterpiece of progressive revelation of divine purposes. God does not open on page one with "For God so loved the world that He gave His only begotten Son, that whosoever believeth in Him should not perish but have everlasting life" (John 3:16, KJV).* Rather, He begins by telling us, "In the beginning God created the heavens and the earth" (Genesis 1:1, KJV).

On page one, we are not ready for John 3:16. We first need to know there is a God, what He is like, that He made us, that we have failed Him and need saving. All those things prepare us to hear that Jesus died for us and that we can trust Him to solve our sin and guilt problems.

In Genesis, God plants all the seeds of the truths He wants to reveal to us. Then slowly, progressively, He builds His story to a climax in redemption and the formation of His Body, the church.

The Bible is divided into the Old Testament and the New Testament. A testament is a covenant, and those divisions refer to the covenants God made with man. The Old Testament was the law made on Mount Sinai with the people of Israel through the man Moses. Preceded by a covenant with Abraham, it gave God's expectations and put man under obligation to obey. The New Testament was a covenant of grace made on

*King James Version.

Calvary with the people of the world through the God-man, Jesus Christ. It showed God's power and mercy and provides us with freedom to live by God's moral law and enjoy His fellowship.

The whole Bible is one picture of progressive plotting of the story of redemption. All that begins in the Old Testament is finished in the New. The following chart shows examples of the relationship between the two testaments. Always, the plan is this: the Old Testament sets the background and pattern, and the New Testament develops and completes the pattern.

RELATIONSHIP OF OLD AND NEW TESTAMENTS
(5 examples)

Old	New
Speaks of origins (Genesis)	Speaks of consummation (Revelation)
Issues prophecies (Genesis 3:15)	Records fulfillments (Galatians 4:4)
Makes statements of truth (Leviticus 17:11)	Explains truth by illustrations (1 Peter 3:18)
Presents pictures of Christ (Numbers 21:9)	Presents reality of Christ (John 3:14-16)
Provides background of spiritual truth (Psalm 23)	Reveals spiritual truth (John 10:1-18)

3. Conclusion. I once heard the conclusion called the "satisfying thump" at the end of a story. Every story needs one. When we study the book of Revelation, we are impressed that here God has given us a magnificent conclusion to His masterpiece of literary and revelatory art. All the resources, problems, and patterns introduced in Genesis are consummated here. A sin-flawed earth is replaced by the new heaven and earth. Sorrow gives way to eternal bliss. Barriers to God-man relationships dissolve into eternal worship of God. Justice sees its final vindication, within the limits of God's merciful character. God's purpose and plan are finally complete, and He

emerges as King of kings and Lord of lords for all eternity.

On all points of literary technique, the Bible rates as a true masterpiece of plot. Its théme is the loftiest and most practical of all themes ever inscribed on the printed page. Where else has God so completely opened His mind and heart to His creatures? Here He shows us His view of Himself, of man as His most valuable work of creation, of nature as ours to care for and enjoy, and of history as the story of His intervention in the affairs of man.

At this point, you are asking, "But how can I ever dig through all those hundreds of pages and find the plot, the view of God, man, nature, and history? I am no student. Where do I begin? Is there some special key to understanding all of this?"

The purpose of this whole course of study is to help you with that. Learning and discovering God's truth will take you a lifetime. He will reveal to you only as much as you can handle for one day at a time. As Aristotle once said, "Learning is no amusement, but is accompanied with pain." Each painful step will yield you some joyful discovery, and gradually the discoveries will combine to give you the overall pictures you seek.

However, there are two keys that can help you see the plot. First, *read panoramically,* as we mentioned in the introduction. You may do this in several ways. You may read the Bible through in a year, following a chart available from several sources. You may read a set number of chapters a day until you reach the end. Personally, I think the best way to get a broad overview of the story line of the Bible is to use the condensed reading plan in Appendix 2. Whatever course of action you settle on, you will find it helpful to consult a Bible time line chart, found in a Bible dictionary, encyclopedia, or other handbook. That will enable you to understand the sequence and relationship of events as you read.

The second key to learning biblical themes is to *look for certain tools that God used to reveal the themes.* Here are five of those tools. I suggest that for each one, you mark off a section in your Bible-reading notebook and record the examples as you find them.

1. The names of God. God began in Genesis 17:1 to reveal Himself through His name "God Almighty." As time went on, He used other names, each revealing some other facet of His character and relationship to man. Those names are a prime example of God's accommodation of Himself to our needs and understanding and as such compose a rich source of progressive revelation of both the plot of Scripture and the nature of God and man.

In your notebook, record each name of God you find, along with its meaning. See Appendix 3 on how to find word and name meanings.

2. The acts of God. God's acts show us truth about His power, His roles in history, His will, and His purposes for man.

In your notebook, record what God did and what His acts reveal about His character and purpose.

3. Statements of God's character. The Bible gives us many statements about the character of God. You might include in this section pictures of God painted by such passages as Psalm 23 (the shepherd) and Luke 15 (the prodigal's father).

Be sure to list the things those pictures and statements tell you about the character of God.

4. Specific commands of a moral nature. The Bible is full of commandments that reveal God's moral nature. Also list the commands that are implied by illustration in Bible stories.

5. Promises of God. You will see in God's promises His view of man, our importance, our strengths, and our weaknesses. It is vital to note the following three questions about each promise:

To whom was it given and under what circumstances?

What conditions are attached to the promise?

Do the promise and its conditions apply to me as well?

As we approach our Bibles to study and learn about ourselves, our world, and our God, we can come with absolute confidence. We are standing on holy ground, before the Book that ranks clearly and indisputably above all books in the world. It is totally reliable, based on solid facts of history, thoroughly practical.

Remember, the Bible can "profitably be used for teaching, for refuting error, for guiding people's lives and teaching them to be holy. This is how the man [or woman] who is dedicated to God becomes fully equipped and ready for any good work" (2 Timothy 3:16, *Jerusalem Bible*).

ASSIGNMENT:

1. Mark off sections in your notebook, as suggested in the text. Begin a habit of using them to record listed observations with all your reading.
2. Fill out the Bible Themes Worksheet.

BIBLE THEMES WORKSHEET

According to the Bible, God is:

_____ (John 4:24)   _____ (Psalm 90:2)

_____ (Isaiah 6:3)   _____ (Revelation 15:3)

_____ (1 John 4:8)   _____ (Psalm 86:15)

_____ (Deuteronomy   _____ (Hebrews 13:8)
              32:4)

_____ (1 Thessalonians   _____ (Isaiah 45:22)
              5:24)

_____ (Isaiah 40:28)   _____ (1 Corinthians
                                               1:25)

According to the Bible, man is:

_____ (Genesis 1:27)   _____ (Genesis 2:7)

_____ (Romans
              3:10-12, 23)   _____ (Jeremiah 31:3)

_____ (Psalm 103:14)

What does Psalm 139 imply about the worth, value, and dignity of man? _____

_____

_____

According to the Bible, nature is:

_____ (John 1:3)

_____ (Psalm 24:1)

_____ (Genesis 1:26, 29)

What does the Bible say about history?

What is the basic purpose of history? (Romans 11:36; Ephesians 4:6) _____

_____

How does God intervene in history?

_____(Deuteronomy 32:8)

_____(Romans 13:1-7)

_____(Exodus 20:1-17)

_____(Psalm 75:6-7)

_____(John 1:14; 3:16)

_____(Psalm 9:16)

LESSON 3

Tools for
Bible Study

When Susan began to study her Bible on her own, she decided that it was a gold mine of truth. "No Bible study books for me," she shouted as she marched into Genesis 1. Several months later, she crawled out at Revelation 22 with an increased accumulation of Bible knowledge, but she was tired, full of questions, and more than a bit confused. She had gained a lot of panoramic surface facts, learned many new commands and promises, and met some fascinating people. To put it all together and apply it in depth to her daily life was something else. She was not sure where to go with what she had found.

By contrast, her friend Julie started her Bible study by taking her checkbook to the local Christian bookstore. Here she purchased an enormous stack of commentaries, dictionaries, and other study guides and helps. When she marched into Genesis 1, she was so loaded down with extra books that she could hardly progress. In fact, she finally decided, halfway through Exodus (about the time Susan was finishing Revelation), that it would take her a lifetime to reach the end. Julie's big problem was that she spent her study time reading what the books had to say about the Bible and read precious little of the Bible itself. All her learning was secondhand. Many of the books she read either led her off the track or did not agree with each other, leaving her more confused and frustrated than educated. The joy of personal discovery totally escaped her.

Many new Bible students make the same kinds of single-track errors. An effective Bible student learns the value of finding a balance between reading the Bible and using Bible study tools. The Bible indeed is an unequaled gold mine of rich, life-changing truth. But without tools, we cannot extricate more than a handful of surface nuggets.

Many people, like Julie, however, never learn to make the tools work for them, because they expect them to do too much for them. Tools do not think for us. They do not answer all our questions. Most of all, they do not replace the Bible.

What then, do they do?

Bible study tools simply assist us in our study of the Bible. Many study guides are available to take you by the hand and lead you step by step through your Bible. Some, such as *What the Bible Is All About,* by Henrietta Mears, provide a schedule, along with notes and explanations to serve as a tour guide on your journey. Others are topical, giving you reading assignments, questions, and notes to help you find all that the Bible tells you on a specific topic. Still others guide you through a single book or smaller passage of the Bible. All kinds of studies have their place and can be helpful. There comes a time in our spiritual growth pattern, however, when we need to dig into the Bible on our own, to do our own study, to make our own discoveries.

What sort of tools do we need then?

The serious gold miner needs Bible study tools that do two things. First, the Bible student needs those tools that give background information to enable one to understand what the Bible says. For example, when we read Psalm 23, the Bible does not stop at the end of verse 1 and give us a detailed account of the life of a shepherd in David's time. Nor does the Bible tell us very much about the Egyptian empire or marriage customs or conversion tables for biblical currency. That is where the tools are useful. Bible dictionaries, encyclopedias, atlases, handbooks, books of customs, even secular history books about ancient non-Hebrew civilizations—those books paint pictures for us of the Hebrew shepherd, the Egyptian pharaohs, the marriage feast, the value of the drachma. As we increase our understanding of those customs and peoples and times that are foreign to our twentieth-century Western culture, we also gain a clearer concept of the psalmist's meaning when he said, "The Lord is my shepherd, I shall not want."

The second thing good Bible study tools will do for us is help us interpret and apply the meaning of Scripture to our own lives. For that purpose, we use books that provide background materials. Topical indexes, modern translations, study Bibles, and commentaries are also helpful.

When you go to the bookstore in search of Bible study tools, the first thing that hits you is the large assortment of books. You cannot simply purchase *a* dictionary. You have to choose between half a dozen dictionaries. You wonder about the difference between an encyclopedia and a dictionary. What is a handbook? How are concordances and topical indexes different? Why so many, many commentaries?

Discovering and using the right tools is a truly exciting experience. Looking for them, on the other hand, can be frustrating. We want to look, then, at the categories and find what each tool can do for us. Then we will talk briefly about some guidelines for choosing and using the tools once we carry our precious packages home and prepare to work.

The first tool we need is a Bible. For a basic text, start with a standard translation such as the King James Version, the *New American Standard Bible,* or the *New International Version.* In addition, it is helpful to have two or three supplementary versions (e.g., *The Amplified Bible* or the Phillips *New Testament in Modern English*).

Bible translations pose a problem because at times they represent the translator's viewpoint. A translator is faced with difficulties of interpretation. Often he finds words in the original languages that cannot be translated precisely. He must either give us a cumbersome array of possibilities to choose from as we read (such as has been done in the *Amplified Bible*), or else make the choices for us. In the interests of clarity and readability, he will usually do the latter.

Paraphrases (e.g., *The Living Bible*) are particularly susceptible to problems here. They actually translate thoughts more than words, and at many points they become more of a translator's commentary than a pure translation. Paraphrases are helpful either to read devotionally or to compare with other versions, particularly with a difficult passage. We should never rely wholly on a paraphrase, however. Multi-version Bibles make translation comparison simple. Several translations are printed in side-by-side columns. Several multi-version Bibles are available either in the New Testament only, or in the whole Bible.

Many people use what are called study Bibles to great advantage. All Bibles that have center or side column chain references are study Bibles of a sort. What I refer to here are Bibles that contain background notes, outlines, maps, charts, dictionaries, pictures, and miscellaneous explanatory articles. They are actually a sort of condensed combination of Bible, dictionary, concordance, encyclopedia, commentary, and atlas all in one volume. Several excellent ones are on the market today.

Although they are an inexpensive, concise, and simple way to go, study Bibles have one basic problem that we need to be aware of. Because they are done by one man or one group of men, and because they are highly condensed, they usually represent a single viewpoint on everything and should not be used to the exclusion of all other study materials.

Dr. R. C. Sproul has suggested in his book *Knowing Scripture* that if you constantly read one study Bible it becomes difficult later on to separate in your mind what was Bible and what was commentary, because you read it all in the same book. I identify with that. When I was growing up, the *Sco-*

field Reference Bible was the most popular edition in our churches. We depended so heavily on Scofield's notes that they came to be the standard by which we judged whether a doctrine was orthodox or not. Scofield was our standard because he was in our Bibles. We did not think of it that way, but that was the psychological effect it had on us. Scofield did a fine job, but his work represented only one man's viewpoint and was not, of course, divinely inspired. We need to be cautious, as Bible students, to separate inspiration from commentary, if we are to find God's truth.

A second tool that is essential is a good concordance. A concordance is a book where you can look up words you know are in the Bible and find the verses where they appear. Many Bibles have short concordances in the back section. Those are usually too limited to be of much value. Others, such as Cruden's, are much more complete and allow you to find many references that you will need. However, the best are the exhaustive ones—Young's and Strong's. In those books, every word that appears in the Bible is included, and each reference where the word occurs is listed, along with a few words of the context to help you find precisely the verse you are looking for. Those two volumes also have dictionaries of both Hebrew and Greek words and a system by which you can find the meanings of the words of Scripture in their original language and see how else the words are used throughout the Bible. See Appendix 3 for instructions in finding word meanings.

A third group of tools that will give you a wealth of helpful background materials includes Bible handbooks, Bible dictionaries, and Bible encyclopedias. A handbook is a concise collection of all sorts of background notes—archaeological discoveries, Bible reading helps, customs, outlines of books, civilization notes, lists of topics, weights and measures, maps, and a host of other bits of information to make Bible study meaningful.

A Bible dictionary contains definitions of Bible topics and names of people and places, and traces their uses through the Scriptures. It also contains outlines of books and sections of the Scriptures, background materials for book studies, biographies, maps, geographical notes, and explanations of customs and cultural oddities. It may or may not be illustrated. Encyclopedias come in both single volumes and in multi-volume sets. They are like extended dictionaries, often filled with drawings, diagrams, maps, and pictures.

```
deliverances
Ps  44: 4 O God: command d' for Jacob.          *3444
delivered  See also DELIVEREDST.
Ge   9: 2 sea; into your hand are they d'.        5414
    14:20 hath d' thine enemies into thy          4042
    25:24 her days to be d' were fulfilled,       3205
    32:16 And he d' them into the hand of         5414
    37:21 and he d' him out of their hands;       5337
Ex   1:19 and are d' ere the midwives come 3205
     2:19 An Egyptian d' us out of the hand 5337
     5:23 neither hast thou d' thy people at       "
    12:27 the Egyptians, and d' our houses.        "
    18: 4 d' me from the sword of Pharaoh:         "
        8 way, and how the Lord d' them,          "
        9 whom he had d' out of the hand           "
       10 who hath d' you out of the hand of       "
       10 of Pharaoh, who hath d' the people       "
Le   6: 2 which was d' him to keep, or in        *6487
        4 which was d' him to keep, or the    *    "
    26:25 and ye shall be d' into the            5414
Nu  21: 3 and d' up the Canaanites; and they     "
       34 I have d' him into thy hand,            "
    31: 5 they were d' out of the thousands 4560
De   2:33 And the Lord our God d' him           5414
       36 the Lord our God d' all unto us:        "
     3: 3 So the Lord our God d' into our         "
     5:22 of stone, and d' them unto me.     *    "
     9:10 And the Lord d' unto me two tables     "
    20:13 God hath d' it into thine hands,    *    "
    21:10 the Lord thy God hath d' them      *    "
    31: 9 and d' it unto the priests the sons     "
Jos  2:24 the Lord hath d' into our hands        "
     9:26 and d' them out of the hand of the 5337
    10: 8 I have d' them into thine hand;      5414
       12 the Lord d' up the Amorites before     "
       19 the Lord your God hath d' them          "
       30 And the Lord d' it also, and the        "
       32 And the Lord d' Lachish into the        "
    11: 8 d' them into the hand of Israel,        "
    21:44 the Lord d' all their enemies into      "
    22:31 ye have d' the children of Israel    5337
    24:10 so I d' you out of his hand.           "
       11 and I d' them into your hand.       5414
J'g  1: 2 I have d' the land into his hand.      "
        4 and the Lord d' the Canaanites         "
     2:14 and he d' them into the hands of        "
       16 which d' them out of the hand of *3467
       18 and d' them out of the hand of    *    "
       23 neither d' he them into the hand   5414
```

Fig. 1. From *Strong's Exhaustive Concordance of the Bible* (Abingdon-Cokesbury Press, 1890), p. 253.

Another tool that is valuable when you want to learn all the Bible has to say on a specific topic is the topical Bible or topical index. There you find outlines of biblical topics and lists of references for Scriptures covering those topics. *Nave's Topical*

Bible is an old standby. In that volume, the Scripture references are not just listed, they are actually written out. Smaller, more compact volumes are now available. They usually list only the references without quoting them. Some also include word definitions and descriptions in addition to the outlines and references.

A fifth category of Bible study tools is commentaries. A commentary is some person's (or group of persons') attempt to interpret and explain the Bible. Commentaries come in single volumes or in large multi-volume sets. Some cover a single book of the Bible. Others, the whole Bible. Commentaries are valuable resources, especially to help you gain insights into difficult passages.

The absolutely essential rule to follow about commentaries is this: Use them only as your last resource. Taken by themselves, they are the lazy person's way to interpret Scripture. At best, using them alone robs the student of the joy of personal discovery. At worst it can mislead and confuse the novice. Using only a commentary means that someone else has done the hard work, and we cash in on his labors. Until I have exhausted all my own powers of research and all my other resources, I determinedly ignore commentaries. Sometimes I come to my own conclusion from my study, or maybe I have several possible interpretations and am not sure which one has the most validity. Then I check all the commentaries on my shelves to get further light before I decide.

Commentaries come in two types—devotional and critical. Devotional commentaries such as the *Matthew Henry Commentary,* emphasize devotional application of each Scripture. Critical commentaries, such as the *Wycliffe Bible Commentary,* examine technical details of background materials, word meanings, and variations in different texts. There is a place for both kinds, but when you are looking for clarification of difficult meanings, where accuracy is more important than emotional reaction, the critical type is usually most valuable.

Finally, you can find several other types of tools for a variety of purposes. There are *atlases* and *books of Bible geography, books of Bible customs, surveys of the whole Bible, surveys of biblical doctrines,* and *books on archaeological discoveries.*

At the end of this lesson, you will find several lists of the books I personally recommend. This is not to say that there are no others that could serve you as well. My list is based on my experience and reflects what I have found to be helpful. Further, new Bible study reference tools are consistently appearing at your bookstore. You will choose your chest of tools to help you meet your own personal study needs. When making your choices, keep the following things in mind:

First, know your needs. How deeply are you prepared to dig? What books can you afford? What do you expect the tools to do for you?

Try, whenever possible, to choose books that serve more than one function. For example, a concordance enables you to find specific verses, but also to find other verses on a related topic and to learn word meanings. A dictionary gives you word meanings, but also background materials, outlines, maps, and many other things.

Also choose those books that enable you to make your own discoveries. Otherwise you could fill your shelves with two multi-volume sets of commentaries and spend your life reading only what other people have to say about the Bible.

Second, know the theological position of the books you choose. That is particularly important if you are buying commentaries or critical studies, which reflect doctrinal biases.

As you read a book you are not sure of, look for attitudes toward inspiration. Does the author believe that all Scripture is God-inspired, or does he simply think the Bible contains God's Word in spots here and there? Look for the author's position on Jesus Christ. Does he present Him as our sole means of salvation, as summarized in Ephesians 2:8-9: "For by grace are ye saved through faith, and that not of yourselves, it is the gift of God. Not of works lest any man should boast" (KJV)? Or is He pictured merely as a great teacher, example, and martyr for a righteous cause?

Third, know your book dealer. His doctrinal position will

often affect the type of books he carries and recommends. If he is Roman Catholic, his outlook will not be the same as a Baptist or charismatic book dealer.

Fourth, know your reading capacity. Some books are *heavy*, with unexplained theological terminology. Others are *deep*, with some theological terminology, but the words have been explained. Still others are *simple* to understand and do not go into any great depth on a topic. Choose for yourself those tools that communicate at a level that makes you stretch your mind, but does not frustrate and discourage you. In the suggested tool lists at the end of this lesson, you will find each one marked with the category level that best describes its readability (H=heavy; D=deep; S=simple).

Fifth, whenever possible borrow books from a church library or friend to examine them before investing money in your own copies.

Sixth, discuss your choices with librarians, book dealers, friends, and your pastor.

Finally, here are five guidelines for using the Bible study tools you collect:

1. Always read your Bible first and last and alongside every tool. Remember, you are not studying what men say about this Book, but what the Book says for itself.

2. Compare different sources of information. Do not take any one source as the final word or authority on every subject.

3. Use commentaries only as your last resource, after you have learned all you can from other sources.

4. Learn the uses and limitations of each tool and do not try to force a book to do what it is not designed to do. For example, a devotional commentary is not a reliable source of information on accurate word meanings. Double check any such entries you find there in a concordance.

5. Do not wait to study until you have a full library of tools. Start small; then add others as you need and can afford them.

When you get ready to bake a cake, you would not think of beginning without a recipe, ingredients, utensils, and an oven.

Similarly, when you start to make a dress, you assemble fabric, pattern, scissors, thread, and a sewing machine. Every job has its list of required tools. Bible study is no exception.

As with cooking and sewing projects, up to a certain point, the more tools you have, the more efficient you can be in getting your job done. However, very few items are truly essential. If all you have is your Bible, you can begin now to go to work. Then, as you are able, add new tools for improving your techniques. The important issue is not how many tools you possess, but how consistently you use the tools you have to help you translate God's truth into daily living skills.

ASSIGNMENT:

Go through the following list of questions and indicate what type of Bible study tools you would use to help you find the answers. Do not look up the answers, just name the tools. In most cases, you could use more than one tool. List as many as you think will do the job. In the suggested tools list that follows, you will find a list of essentials, particularly three tools that are crucial—concordances, a topical index, and Bible handbooks. As you do this assignment, use those three first, wherever possible, before checking into other kinds of resources.

(A complete list of answers may be found following the list of suggested tools.)

BIBLE STUDY TOOLS WORKSHEET

What *tools* would you use to find each of the following?

1. List of Scriptures on topic of worship.

2. Meaning of biblical weights and measures.

3. Name of country that was world political power in days of Isaiah.

4. Meaning of the word translated "faith" in Galatians 5:22. Is the same original word used for faith in 1 Corinthians 13:13?

5. Who was Abigail?

6. What psalms were called the *hallel* psalms and why?

7. How did ancient Hebrews educate their children?

8. List all the references where the Beatitudes are given.

9. What historical events happened in the 400 years between the Old and New Testaments?

10. Who wrote the book of Judges?

11. To whom did Jesus say, "It is hard for thee to kick against the pricks"?

12. Where was Sychar located?

13. Who was the god of Moab and how was he worshiped?

14. Where do you find the verse "He was wounded for our transgressions"?

SUGGESTED TOOLS LISTS

LIST 1—Essential

D 1. *Strong's Exhaustive Concordance of the Bible,* by James Strong. Abingdon Press. (Comes in two forms. One is the standard concordance; the other contains a keyword comparison section, where you can learn what words are used to translate the original Hebrew or Greek in five of the modern language versions—*Revised Standard Version, New English Bible, Jerusalem Bible, New American Standard,* and *New International Version.*)

D or *Young's Analytical Concordance of the Bible,* by Robert Young. Eerdman's Publishing Company.

S 2. *Eerdman's Handbook to the Bible,* edited by David and Patricia Alexander. Eerdman's Publishing Company.

S 3. *Nave's Topical Bible,* by Orville J. Nave. Moody Press.

S or *The New Compact Topical Bible.* Zondervan Publishing House.

S or *The Bible Index Pocketbook.* Harold Shaw Publishers. (This one is small, purse size, an excellent quick reference to carry with you. Highly recommended.)

LIST 2—Strongly Recommended

D 1. *The Word Study New Testament and Concordance,* by George Wigram and Ralph Winter. Tyndale House.

2. *The Wycliffe Bible Encyclopedia,* by Charles F. Pfeiffer, Howard F. Vos, and John Rea. Moody Press.

S 3. *Exploring the Scriptures,* by John Phillips. Moody Press.

S 4. *Strange Scriptures that Perplex the Western Mind,* by Barbara Bowen. Eerdman's Publishing Company.

S 5. *Manners and Customs,* by Fred Wight. Moody Press.

D 6. *Manners and Customs,* by James Freeman. Logos International.

LIST 3—Recommended

D 1. *Major Bible Themes,* by Lewis Sperry Chafer and John F. Walvoord. Zondervan Publishing House.

S 2. *Life of Christ in Stereo,* by Johnston M. Cheney. Western Baptist Press.

D 3. *New Testament Times,* by Merrill C. Tenney. Eerdman's Publishing Company.

S 4. *The Bible As History,* by Werner Keller. William Morrow and Co. Paperback edition, Bantam Books.

S 5. *Understanding the Bible,* by John R. Stott. Zondervan Publishing House.

LIST 4—Helpful

D 1. *The Wycliffe Bible Commentary,* edited by Everett F. Harrison and Charles F. Pfeiffer. Moody Press.

D 2. *The New Bible Dictionary,* by J. D. Douglas. Eerdman's Publishing Company.

D   or *Unger's Bible Dictionary,* by Merrill F. Unger. Moody Press.

D   or *Zondervan Pictorial Bible Dictionary.* Zondervan Publishing House.

D 3. *Wycliffe Historical Geography of Bible Lands,* by Charles F. Pfeiffer and Howard F. Vos. Moody Press.

S 4. *The Macmillan Bible Atlas,* by Yohanan Aharoni and Michael Avi-Yonah. Macmillan Company.

LIST 5—Others

D 1. *Zondervan Pictorial Encyclopedia of the Bible,* Merrill C.
&   Tenney, editor. Zondervan Publishing House. (Excellent
H   work, but in five volumes and expensive.)

S 2. *All the Women of the Bible,* by Edith Deen. Harper & Row.

S 3. *Great Verses Through the Bible,* by F. B. Meyer. Zondervan Publishing House.

D 4. *Matthew Henry's Commentary,* by Matthew Henry. Zondervan Publishing House.

BIBLE STUDY TOOLS WORKSHEET ANSWERS

1. Topical Bible (or index); concordance; study Bible
2. Handbook; book of customs; dictionary; encyclopedia; study Bible
3. Handbook; encyclopedia; dictionary; atlas; Bible survey; study Bible; commentary
4. Concordance
5. Concordance; dictionary; encyclopedia; handbook
6. Study Bible; handbook; dictionary; encyclopedia

7. Encyclopedia; dictionary
8. Concordance; handbook; study Bible; marginal reference
9. Handbook; encyclopedia; commentary; Bible survey; study Bible
10. Handbook; dictionary; encyclopedia; Bible survey; study Bible; commentary
11. Concordance
12. Handbook; atlas; Bible maps; dictionary; encyclopedia
13. Handbook; encyclopedia; dictionary
14. Concordance.

LESSON 4
Interpreting the Bible

When you assemble all the ingredients and utensils needed to make a soufflé, you still need one more thing to ensure success—a recipe. If you do not know about separating eggs or making white sauce or baking at the right temperature with the soufflé casserole sitting in a pan of water, what you serve your family may not at all resemble a soufflé, regardless of how fresh the ingredients or how perfect the tools.

The same is true with Bible study. You begin with the perfect ingredients—the Bible itself. Although you have the finest tools, you may still encounter difficulty learning precisely what it means. The Bible is perhaps the most misunderstood Book on earth. Most false religions that have arisen out of a Christian background and use the Bible as a secondary text are based on misinterpretations of Scripture. It is a well-known fact that you can make the Bible say anything you want it to say simply by combining, interposing, and culling to fit your fancy.

If we are to get a firm grasp of the overall message of the Bible and of the details of its application to our lives, we need to learn to follow certain rules of interpretation. In this lesson, we want to look first at those rules. Then we will examine a simple, basic study method that enables us to study by them.

Read the Bible systematically, similar to the way you read any other book. Which other book on your library shelves would you pick up and let it fall open where it chances, or put your finger on a spot and start reading there, in order to gain wisdom? That is not the way to read a book—any book. Although we do not always start on the first page, we at least read most books in logical, connected units. Sometimes we want to pursue certain topics or time periods that do not require us to go back to the beginning before we can understand them. But we need to read with some sense of continuity, system, and purpose, not just in hop-skip-jump style.

Consider the overall purpose of the Bible. Relate all your studies to an awareness that the Bible is basically a declaration of God's person and works, especially as they concern the redemption of man. In other words, we do not go to the Bible to learn all there is to know about ancient history. Rather, we go there to learn how ancient history fits into God's plan of redemption.

Learn to consider the special characteristics and messages of individual books of the Bible. Each book has its own slant, its own emphasis, its own original audience, its own way of saying things.

For example, as we read the four gospels (Matthew, Mark, Luke, and John), we hear four different men telling us the same story, but with a variety of themes and choice of details. In the book of Matthew, we read about the kingship of Christ. That is why Matthew's gospel includes the story of the worshiping magi and the many ways Jesus' life fulfilled Old Testament prophecies of a Messiah King in Israel. Mark's gospel talks about the servanthood of Christ and emphasizes the ways Christ served others. Mark gives us the well-known text "For even the Son of man came not to be ministered unto, but to minister, and to give his life a ransom for many" (Mark 10:45, KJV). Luke presents the humanity of Christ. He shares many details of the human circumstances of His birth and pictures of His humanness. Finally, John focuses on Jesus' deity and gives us some of the deepest passages of teaching that show

Jesus Christ as the earthly, human manifestation of God.

Knowing the character of each book is essential. It is imperative to know that Ecclesiastes is not to be taken as a series of declarations of God's patterns for our lives. Rather, it was the structured reminiscence of a bitter old man who had known God in younger years, but lived the bulk of his life on the edge of spiritual rebellion.

Consider the writer's purpose. Learn who the writer was. Where did he come from? What customs were peculiar to his day? How did people react to spiritual truth in his day? What was considered right and wrong? What were the immediate needs of his original readers? What was the historical background of the book? What were political, economic, and social conditions? All those things are important to our proper understanding of any book of the Bible. When I can put myself, for instance, in the shoes of Abigail (see 1 Samuel 25), I have a much better understanding of how her circumstances were like mine or different from mine. That enables me to see how God wants to deal with me in my difficulties with ungodly relatives.

Consider the context. Suppose a friend is planning to marry a godless young man who has a long list of illicit sex credits. Her parents, counselors, friends, and pastor have all warned her that such action is dangerous. They remind her of the clear biblical command not to be "bound together with unbelievers; for what partnership have righteousness and lawlessness?" (2 Corinthians 6:14). Anxious to justify herself and find divine sanction for her rebellious plans, your friend digs around and comes up with an obscure verse buried deep in the Old Testament minor prophets. "The Lord said to Hosea, 'Go, take to yourself a wife of harlotry' " (Hosea 1:2).

"God told His prophet to marry a godless harlot," she defends her decision, "so why can't I marry this man?"

That verse was never issued as a command to Christians to use when choosing a life partner. Read the context and you learn that it was a one-of-its-kind incident planned by God as an object lesson of His marital-like love for the people of Israel. When your friend distorts it to mask her rebellion, she will encounter only disaster.

Consider other Scriptures on the same theme. Compare Scripture with Scripture. The Bible is not arranged as a topical treatise, where Genesis tells us all about sin, Exodus all about God, Leviticus all about prayer, and so on. Each book has a theme, a main emphasis. But just because the theme of Leviticus is worship does not mean that Leviticus tells us all there is to know about worship. Rather, worship verses are scattered liberally through all the books from Genesis on through to a glorious climax of worship in Revelation. God wants us to read the whole Book. If you want to learn all He has to say about anything, you have to read the whole thing. Furthermore, He wants us to realize that all truth is interrelated and permeates every area of life.

As you compare the Scriptures for overall godly viewpoints, remember that no part of the Bible ever conflicts with any other part. If two statements appear to conflict, you have misread something somewhere along the line.

Consider the exact meaning of important words. There are many words in the original Hebrew and Greek texts that simply have no precise English equivalents. Here is where comparing translations can help you. Remember that the most reliable tool for checking the accuracy of word meanings is the exhaustive concordance with its Hebrew and Greek dictionaries.

Avoid personal prejudices and biases when reading and studying the Bible. Come with a mind and heart that are open to what God wants to tell you, not with preconceived ideas of what you want Him to tell you.

Wherever possible, interpret the Scriptures literally. Literal interpretation is not always possible, as we will note in the next rule. Parts of the Bible are not meant to be taken literally. For example, when we read that "God's arm is not shortened" (Isaiah 59:1, KJV), we must not assume that God has a flesh-and-blood arm such as we have. On the other hand, when He tells us, "Do not lie to one another" (Colossians 3:9), He means we are not, under any circumstances, to lie to one another.

Some people feel that every Scripture passage should be interpreted spiritually, that some deep mystical, spiritual meaning should be attached to it, that it should not be taken at face value. That is dangerous thinking. By so doing, we can spiritualize away a lot of practical truth until the Bible no longer speaks to us. Instead, we shape it into our own mold and make it say whatever we want it to say.

The Bible gives to us God's clear, absolute, and propositional truth. It does not become His truth only as we apply it to our lives. It *is* His truth, regardless of what we do with it. God will one day judge us all on the basis of what He said, not the spiritual meaning we assigned to His words. Hence we need to take it as it is and not attempt to change it around to satisfy our individual fancies and life-styles.

Be familiar with the literary devices used in the Bible. If you are interested in pursuing a literary study of the Bible, you will find a book in the Supplementary Reading List (Appendix 4) to help you. For our purposes here it is sufficient to define the term *literary devices* and to mention and illustrate a few of the most frequently used ones.

Literary devices are figures of speech and forms of expression by which God accommodates Himself to our understanding and paints pictures to insure that we grasp His meaning. One of the most frequently used devices is *personification,* which takes an impersonal object and assigns to it characteristics of human personality. ("The trees of the field will clap their hands," Isaiah 55:12.) If we interpret such expressions literally, we are in trouble. Instead, we read the imagery, see the implied meaning, and recognize that Isaiah is simply emphasizing the fact that even all of nature rejoices before her Creator.

Another common device is *parallelism,* which is the basis for Hebrew poetry. Here a statement is made, then it is made again in a different way.

A wise man will hear and increase in learning,
And a man of understanding will acquire wise counsel.

Proverbs 1:5

Both statements say the same thing, but in slightly different words. It is easy, if we do not understand the principle of parallelism, to get carried away trying to interpret such verses minutely. Many people do that and attempt to discover some additional shade of meaning in each repetition of thought. Often that leads to the construction of monstrously complicated doctrines that are not intended at all.

See lesson 9, "Studying a Poem," for further explanation of Hebrew poetry and parallelism.

A *metaphor* is another literary device in which the writer substitutes a picture word for some philosophical concept or abstract idea. When Jesus said, "I am the Door" (John 10:7), He did not mean that He was a literal door. He called Himself a door because He wanted us to understand that as a door opens up access to a house, so He opens the way into the kingdom of heaven.

Parables are literary devices in the form of practical earthly stories that illustrate spiritual truth. These are not allegories, such as *Pilgrim's Progress,* where each detail represents some specific truth. Each parable tells us one main truth. If we try to make each detail mean something spiritual, we may end up with an atrocious monster of an interpretation. For more on this subject, see lesson 10 ("Studying a Parable").

One more literary device is a *proverb.* Proverbs are short, pithy statements that communicate succinctly and memorably gems of common sense wisdom, as seen from God's point of view.

Do not build a doctrine on the example of one story or verse alone. We read in the Bible that when sin became the unruly norm for society, God told Noah to build an ark (Genesis 6-9). We must not conclude that in our decadent society, we too need to build an ark. God's stories are not all concluded with a command to "go and do thou likewise."

Doctrines and patterns for living are taught in the teaching passages of the Bible, which serve as commentaries to the stories. We must learn to read all parts of Scripture, then put them together to form one big coordinated picture. Actually, we do not discover truth of any kind in single isolated passages of the Bible. Doctrines are understood as we compare Scripture with Scripture—teaching with teaching, and teaching with stories.

Observe the difference between the letter of God's laws and the spirit of those laws. The letter of the law commands, "Thou shalt" or "Thou shalt not!" The spirit of the law says, "I have compassion and understand where you are coming from, so I will help you meet the demands of My law." We must find a godly balance between condemnation and forgiveness. We must not use God's laws to clobber one another into submission to our specific ways of interpreting God's Word. At the same time, we do not want to become so wishy-washy that we excuse sin by saying, "Oh, it's the spirit of the law to remember that God loves us no matter whether we obey Him or not."

When we begin tossing out laws as of no consequence, God is offended. The truth is that God loves us too much to eliminate even one of His laws. He is also anxious to forgive us when we break those laws and genuinely repent. Some of God's laws are difficult to interpret and apply. It takes a lifetime, with some. Further, if it is so difficult to discern the fine lines for ourselves, we certainly need to be controlled by the spirit of the law in setting expectations of our brothers and sisters.

Recognize the need for a balance between personal study and receiving instruction from others. Just because you are studying this book and learning to study the Bible for yourself does not mean that you no longer need to attend church or neighborhood Bible studies or study the Bible with your family. None of us will ever be the final authority on anything that we have discovered in our studies. God has given us each other in His Body in order to encourage one another, to help us interpret

His truth, and to keep us from going off on dangerous tangents.

Become personally involved in what you study. Take everything as a personal message to you, not just a vague statement of universal knowledge and the big broad "will of God" (whatever that is). God expects us to get actively involved with Him and His Word as we study. Are there promises in the passage I read today? Does it reveal some pattern of thought in my life that needs changing? Maybe some habit I need to get rid of? Is there some command for me to obey? How will my life be different because I have studied this passage today? If our lives never change through our Bible study, then we have wasted a lot of precious time in a purely academic adventure with no important function.

Keep Jesus Christ central in all your studies. Biblical prophecy becomes a hobby with a lot of people. It holds a special fascination for the human mind, hungry as we all are to know about the future and to solve its detailed problems.

I once heard a Bible teacher relate how we can tell whether we are properly using Bible prophecy or whether we are abusing it. "When you study prophecy," he said, "if you get intrigued with the details and with the prophetic plan and making your chart so you can predict precisely what is going to happen and when, you have abused it. If on the other hand, your reaction is to fall before the Lord and pray, 'Oh, God, I need You so much; I want to be more submissive to Jesus,' then you have used prophecy rightly."

The same principle applies to other areas of Bible study and its application—current moral issues, controversial systems of doctrine, and the like. No matter what we study, if it brings us more and more into subjection to Jesus Christ, we have used it as God intended. Whenever Bible study becomes an end in itself or makes us feel that we are now ready to set the whole world straight, we have abused it.

This, then, is one of the most important of all laws about interpreting Scripture. For our attitudes toward the truth, one another, and primarily toward Jesus Christ are the basis for all we will ever learn from the Bible.

With those rules as a foundation, we want to experiment with a simple, basic method for interpreting the Bible. It is the skeleton on which we will build all other methods. It consists of four questions we ask of each passage.

1. What does this passage say? Use all your senses to discover everything in the verses before you. On the worksheet at the end of this lesson, you will have an opportunity to practice this method. In the first slot, you will jot down everything you observe as you read the assigned verses. Who are the people? Who wrote the passage? To whom? What places are involved? What are the circumstances of the writing, the reader, the story?

Look also for repeated words and phrases. Whenever a word or phrase is repeated many times, we can be sure that it has special significance. God's method is to repeat things for emphasis. For example, a constantly recurring phrase in Exodus is "I am the Lord." The repetition helps us to identify the theme of the book—God called Israel to be His special people.

2. What does this passage mean? What was God trying to say to the people this was first written to, or to the people involved in this story? In order to answer those kinds of questions, you may have to do some background study. If you do not understand much about Egypt in Moses' day, you will not fully understand why the plagues made such an impact on the Egyptians (Exodus 7-12). We all can imagine, for example, how uncomfortable it would be to have frogs in bed with us, in our kitchen, and underfoot everywhere we turn. If we know, further, that the Egyptians worshiped the frog, the significance of the plague of the frogs suddenly deepens, and we can see God using frogs to teach the important lesson "I am the Lord."

3. What does this passage mean to me? In my study of the plagues, I know that God was showing His superiority over the Egyptian gods. How can such a remote historical event apply to my life?

As I think through the spiritual implications of the event in the lives of the Egyptians, I get a clue for myself. Perhaps I, too, have held something in a treasured position in my life, and I need to see that God is supreme over that thing or person. This passage reveals to me that the thing or person that occupies first place in my life and affections has actually become like a god to me.

4. How will my life be different because I have studied these verses? This is the part of Bible study that pinches. If we do all the other steps and leave this one undone, the Bible will never have a genuine impact on our lives. Remember, God's Word is not a curiosity piece for us to read and fill our heads with knowledge. Rather, it is a living, motivating Word that will change our lives if we diligently apply all the rules for proper interpretation and give God a chance to speak to us.

ASSIGNMENT:

1. Study John 6:1-15, using the Basic Four-Question Worksheet.
2. Record ideas for future studies, as they come to you, on the Bible Study Ideas Worksheet at conclusion of lesson 1.

Note: Following is a sample of the worksheet you will be doing. It includes the things we have talked about from Exodus 8:1-15. Study it so that you will understand better how to do your own assignment. Instructions in the sample are enclosed in parentheses. Sample entry materials are italicized.

BASIC FOUR-QUESTION WORKSHEET
(Sample)

Scripture Passage: *Exodus 8:1-15*

WHAT DOES IT SAY? *Among other things, God sent frogs to overrun Egypt because of Pharaoh's stubborn refusal to let the people of Israel go.*
(Other things to note in this story will be the characters—Pharaoh, Moses, and Aaron. The place is Egypt. The circumstances are the slavery of Israelites, Pharaoh's broken promises, Moses'

obedience, and the plague of frogs and what it was like. One repeated phrase that has significance is "Let My people go." In this sheet, we have picked a single track of thought to trace through our study.)

WHAT DOES IT MEAN? *Egyptians worshiped the frog. So, when frogs overran the land, not only were they a nuisance, but they were God's message to the people that the God of Israel was superior to all the gods of Egypt (see v. 10). He planned it so that the last memory of their frog god from this occasion was "the land stank" (v. 14, KJV).*

WHAT DOES IT MEAN TO ME? *Those stacks of books I have been reading lately have become too important to me. Could they be like a false god? Perhaps God wants me to get rid of them so that I can worship Him more completely. Is He really the Lord of my reading life?*

HOW WILL MY LIFE BE DIFFERENT BECAUSE I HAVE STUDIED THIS? *I will spend more time reading the Bible. I will be more selective about the books I read. I will stop my practice of neglecting some of the needs of my family while I spend excessive amounts of time reading all the books I want to read.*

BASIC FOUR-QUESTION WORKSHEET

SCRIPTURE PASSAGE:

WHAT DOES IT SAY?

WHAT DOES IT MEAN?

WHAT DOES IT MEAN TO ME?

HOW WILL MY LIFE BE DIFFERENT BECAUSE I HAVE STUDIED THIS?

LESSON 5

Devotional Bible Study

The grandfather clock strikes six from the entryway, as your husband dashes out the door for work. You have thirty minutes until you must call the children—thirty choice minutes for uninterrupted solitude before you go into orbit for the day. So you sit at the breakfast table and sip a cup of strong coffee while you read your Bible passage for the morning. Training and experience have taught you that somewhere in these verses God has tucked away a practical, personal message designed to guide you all day long. So you read until something grabs you, then meditate on it a bit, offer a few words of fleeting prayer punctuated by a hasty final "Amen," lay down your Bible, and rush off to call the kids.

That type of Bible study is the most commonly practiced method there is. In fact, it is the only method most people know anything about. We call it devotional study—and it can be fine for starters.

Devotional study is actually very important. God uses it to say many things to us. Every study we do should be partly devotional—at least in its application. Devotional studies accomplish three of the main goals of all Bible study: (1) They inspire us to worship God. (2) They give us something practical to live by. (3) They speak personally and intimately to our hearts.

Effective devotional studies, however, are more complex than they appear. Because they help us find God's spiritual messages, we tend to think that they do not demand much intellectual work. Since they involve our hearts, they are more emotional than intellectual, and surely, we reason, they can be done rather easily by just turning our spirits and emotions loose in the presence of Holy Writ. When we approach these studies with that attitude, they become little more than the cursory reading we have earlier described as walking down a pathway, picking up loose treasures that glitter up at us from the surface of the ground.

The hidden treasures that we need to sustain us at the deeper levels of living must be dug up with minds and hearts working together. Surprisingly, when we learn to use our minds to research biblical backgrounds, to discover difficult word meanings, to get acquainted with literary techniques, biblical characters, and God Himself, we find our hearts responding at a more intense level than we ever dreamed possible.

It works a bit like going to an art museum to view the works of a famous painter. If I have no understanding of art theory or appreciation, my enthusiasm for the exhibit will be limited to what pleases my native, unrefined, aesthetic senses at first glance. If I have studied line and color and design, if I know something about the artistic process and the life of the painter, I will react with my heart and linger long as I make dozens of exciting discoveries in each item displayed.

Likewise with the Bible. If I have difficulty understanding what a passage says, at best, I will not be able to decide what it should mean to me or how to apply it. At the worst, I may pick up erroneous meanings and misapply the whole thing.

We have put devotional studies at the beginning of our sequence of methods in this book, not because they are the simplest, but because of the devotional nature of all studies. You will benefit most from this course if you keep the goals and techniques of devotional study in mind as you work your way through all the other lessons.

Before we examine the specific devotional study method, let me suggest two invaluable tools that have helped thousands of Bible students to be effective in this type of study.

One is a spiritual journal. When I say journal, you probably think of a diary. Perhaps you have tried at some time to keep some sort of running record of your life. "Today I went to the store and bought ten pounds of potatoes on sale for 89¢." Or, "Today I started a new management course at work." Before long, you found this endless recording of mundane history to be tedious and hardly worth the investment of your precious time. So, you gave it up as an impractical idea.

I am not talking about a diary. A journal is different. While your diary reminds you of what you did or experienced, your journal reports how you reacted, how you felt, what you learned, or what new questions you began to ask from those random events. The day you found the potatoes on sale, your journal says, "Thank You, Lord, for leading me to that special sale. It's so neat the way You cooperate with my efforts to be a good steward of resources You provide."

I began keeping a spiritual journal when I was in high school. Since then, I have passed through periods of months or years when all my recordings were sketchy and sporadic. For the past fifteen years or so, my journal has been one of my most treasured companions. I do not write in it every day. Sometimes I go for a week without recording a line. At other times, I write pages every day without a break. It depends on what goes on inside of me.

In my journal, I tell God how much I love Him, confess my weaknesses, and plead with Him for help. Sometimes I admit that I am angry with Him. Other days, I just say, "I am feeling something today—not sure what, but the feeling is intense. Help me to deal with it, Lord."

How much or how little you record is not important. What is important is that you set something down on paper. That is because our minds are full of half-formed opinions, ideas, and scriptural messages. As long as they stay unformed, they remain disconnected, vague, puzzling, even troubling. They will never be fully formed until we put them into words. Our journal offers us a choice opportunity to do that. Even if we ramble all over the pages, the process of verbalizing our thoughts helps us to shape and clarify them.

In the process, we also solve many of our problems. Have you ever had a friend who was a good listener? When you take a problem to her, you can talk it out and come away convinced that she helped you. Probably you found your own answer by verbalizing your way through the situation. A journal is that sort of friend. Its empty pages, like open ears, invite us to share our deepest needs, our honest hangups, our random thoughts, and the bits and pieces of divine truth we are gleaning through our Bible study. Many times we lay down our pens and close the book, realizing that the problem has been solved.

Most important of all, the spiritual journal helps us to appreciate the greatness of God. When I go back and reread my journal, I can trace the progression of God's work in my life. My personal record reminds me once more that He is a faithful, provident Father. I respond with worship and adoration to Him for caring enough to bring me through my problems, lead me out of my foolishness and depressions, and answer prayers I had even forgotten about praying.

Another tool for effective devotional study is a pencil for marking your Bible. Some people mistakenly believe that the Bible is too holy to be marked. Actually, the paper itself is not holy, only its message. The Bible is not an icon or a religious relic to be venerated. Rather, it is a workbook to be written in, cried over, used until its pages yellow and become frayed around the edges.

One pastor writes, "A marked Bible shows a Christian in transit. . . . Notations in the Bible are like notches in the Rock of Ages. They show how far up we have scaled its face and what we have seen."[1]

How should we mark our Bibles? It is of little value to get

1. John Gilmore, "Make Your Mark in the Bible," *Eternity*, March 1974, p. 33.

so excited about the idea that we underline almost every verse we read. What will help us for later reference is to mark the things that have special importance to us, things we want to recall more easily or locate quickly, key words and ideas that help us trace a theme through some passage or through the entire Bible.

One way to mark effectively is to use different colors for different types of markings. For example, you might use red for promises, green for commands. We can put letter clues in our margins (e.g., "C" in the margin beside commands; "P" beside promises). You may underline some kinds of things; circle others; use different kinds of lines—straight, wavy, double. You can use the margins to record brief sermon notes, pertinent quotations, personal reactions, dates, and circumstances when a passage speaks to you in some special way.

Another practical idea is to make lists of passages and verses that are helpful for specific types of need. When you find verses that speak to the needs of grief, trial, temptation, decision-making, jot the references in your list on one of the blank pages at the back of your Bible. Make lists of promises, special instructions for prayer, or any other topic you might want to refer to often.

Once you begin to approach your Bible as a workbook and look for creative ways to make it practical, you will find many things to fill in the blank spaces.

Learning to keep a spiritual journal and to mark our Bibles teaches us to think devotionally about God and His Word and prepares us to get the most out of our devotional studies. As we approach the actual devotional studies, we will be drawing on our accumulated knowledge up to the present and attempting to grasp God's practical messages for us, based on that level of knowledge. Sometimes we need to look up a word or a cross reference, or branch off and find out what else the Bible has to say on a specific topic, in order to increase our understanding of "What does it say?" But in general, this is not a technical research kind of study.

Ten years from now, when we come back to the same passage we studied today, we will no doubt have increased our technical knowledge of the passage so that we will see things in it we cannot see today. Fine. For now, we want to dig out what we can find for today and be content with that as God's revealed truth for our use here and now.

For your help in doing a devotional study, I have provided a worksheet. This is not the one and only way to study devotionally. But it contains the elements that are most important to help achieve the goals stated in the beginning of this chapter. It is wise, when doing devotional studies, to limit yourself to a small number of verses and to look for one or two main ideas throughout. Keep it simple and direct.

As you begin this study, remember three things:

1. Observe the rules for study and interpretation. Use tools only as needed, never as substitutes for the Bible itself.

2. If you are studying these lessons in a class, do not compare results with the idea of judging who is the best student or most spiritual Christian. Do not expect, either, that every member will get the same answers on the worksheet. Particularly in a devotional study, you will each receive from God those things that are tailored to meet your individual, immediate needs.

3. If there are blanks you cannot fill in, move on. If you do not come up with anything as profound as you expected, that is fine, too. Do what you can, learn what you can, and simply thank God for what He has helped you to glean for today.

Following, you will find a sample worksheet with instructions and a blank worksheet for your assignment. Study the sample sheet first. Instructions are enclosed in parentheses.

Sample entry materials are italicized.

ASSIGNMENT:

1. Using the devotional study worksheet, do a devotional study of Psalm 37:1-11.
2. Record on the Bible Study Ideas Worksheet at the end of lesson 1 any new ideas for devotional Bible studies you may want to do in the future.

DEVOTIONAL BIBLE STUDY WORKSHEET
(Sample)

SCRIPTURE PASSAGE:

 Matthew 6:24-34 DATE: *April 18, 1983*

PRAYER FOR GUIDANCE: (We may not need to write this out, but we must never begin a study without taking time to pray for guidance.)

Dear Lord, give me a true openness to You and Your message in these verses.

I. HEART-SEARCHING: (In all devotional study we should search our hearts. Such searching always hurts. It rarely produces things that please us. This should encourage us, for until we find our weaknesses, blind spots, and points of rebellion, we cannot correct them and grow.)

What is my attitude to material things? Five times these verses mention the folly of anxiety over things — vv. 25, 27, 28, 31, 34. What is my attitude to spiritual matters? — v. 33.

CONFESSION: (Unless we erect roadblocks to the Holy Spirit and refuse to listen, confession comes as a natural result of heart-searching. If God speaks to me about a thing, I dare not go looking for anything else until I stop and deal with the problem at hand.)

I must admit, I often trust my husband's paycheck more than Your providential love to keep me from anxiety.

II. MEDITATION: (Here we ponder certain things in the passage that need extra thought. What great things has God done? What is the meaning of a particular sin, command, or promise mentioned here? Am I guilty of the sin in this passage? Do I need the promise? What logic does God give for the point He is making?)

(1) *Life is more important than things — v. 25 — plants and animals — vv. 26-30.* (2) *Anxiety won't help anything — v. 27.* (3) *Anxiety is a heathen activity — vv. 31-32.*

THANKSGIVING: (When we have meditated on God and His message, we are ready to thank Him for some problem revealed, promise received, or new truth perceived about God.)

Thank You, heavenly Father, for Your enormous investment in my daily material needs.

III. WORSHIP: (All devotional studies should lead us to an experience of worship, in our hearts if not on paper. Worship grows naturally out of meditation and thanksgiving.)

Such a perfectly provident Father, O God, You deserve the ultimate degree of my trust, confidence, and adoration.

PRAYER AND INTERCESSION: (Worship leads us to see things from God's perspective so we can begin to pray effectively.)

Pray for material and spiritual needs of unemployed, ill, young breadwinners, oppressed, catastrophe victims.

IV. INSTRUCTIONS: (Here we get very specific. Based on all God has shown us in steps 1-3 above, exactly what is He asking us to do today? He has a specific design and purpose for our study time each day, and we must be quiet enough in heart to hear what He is saying. It is vital that we verbalize those things so there is no chance for them to remain half-formed, vague impressions in our minds.)

(1) Serve God, not material wealth or daily needs — v. 24. (2) Don't be anxious — vv. 25, 27, 28, 31, 34. (3) Make His kingdom and personal godliness first priority — v. 33. (4) Refuse to worry about problems tomorrow may bring — v. 34.

COMMITMENT: (Logical result of verbalizing instructions. Writing down a commitment has potent implications. Psychologically, it is much more difficult to renege on a written commitment than a spoken one. Further, once it is recorded, it is there for us to refresh our minds later when we may have become careless about living up to it.)

Lord, with Your help, I will concentrate on pleasing You and trust You with the material results.

KEY VERSE OR THOUGHT: (Choose a short phrase or verse that you can learn easily and remember as you need it to remind you of your commitment and God's power to help you keep that commitment.)

"Why are you anxious?"

DEVOTIONAL BIBLE STUDY WORKSHEET

SCRIPTURE PASSAGE: DATE:

PRAYER FOR GUIDANCE:

 I. HEART-SEARCHING:

    CONFESSION:

 II. MEDITATION:

    THANKSGIVING:

III. WORSHIP:

    PRAYER AND INTERCESSION:

IV. INSTRUCTIONS:

    COMMITMENT:

KEY VERSE OR THOUGHT:

SUGGESTED DEVOTIONAL STUDY PASSAGES

This is not a complete list, but just a few passages for starters.

Deuteronomy 6:1-15
Joshua 1:1-9
Psalm 15:1-5
Proverbs 3:1-12
Isaiah 1:16-27
Isaiah 12:1-6
Isaiah 40:28-31
Isaiah 55:6-13
Jeremiah 29:11-14
Lamentations 3:22-26
Matthew 5:1-12
Matthew 10:16-42

Matthew 11:28-30
Luke 10:1-6
Luke 14:25-33
John 10:1-14
John 14:1-6
John 15:12-17
Romans 12:13-21
1 Corinthians 6:15-20
2 Corinthians 4:1-4
Galatians 5:16-24
Ephesians 6:1]8
Philippians 2:1-11

Colossians 3:12-17
1 Thessalonians 4:9-12
1 Timothy 2:1-4
1 Timothy 6:17-19
Hebrews 4:14-16

Hebrews 12:5-13
James 3:1-18
1 Peter 4:7-11
1 John 1:5-10
Revelation 5:1-14

LESSON 6

Paraphrasing Scripture

If I could recite the names of the books of the Bible forward and backward and could tell you who wrote each book, why he wrote it, and what it contains; if I knew Bible geography from Mount Carmel to the Nile and from Mesopotamia to Rome and knew something about every person mentioned in the Bible; if I could give you detailed outlines and proof texts for every Bible doctrine and understood all the intricate mysteries of Bible prophecy; even if I had the Bible memorized from cover to cover but never allowed it to challenge my point of view or change my life-style, all my super knowledge would help me about as much as a college degree in the midst of an earthquake or a family quarrel.

What you have just read is a paraphrase of one of the most familiar verses in the Bible—1 Corinthians 13:1. It does what a paraphrase is supposed to do, and it shows you what paraphrases can do to help you learn to study your Bible.

First, a paraphrase takes the words of Scripture, asks what they mean and "so what?" Then it rewrites them in words that remind us what we should be doing about what we know.

Second, a paraphrase takes whatever Bible knowledge we may have and helps us decide how God wants us to handle such issues as divorce, abortion, government, and public schools. It also helps us learn God's approach to practical problems—how to speak gently when we feel like screaming, how to be honest with ourselves and our nosy friends, and how to prevent a competitive spirit from destroying our homes.

Writing a paraphrase is like keeping a journal. It helps us crystallize our thinking and commit ourselves on paper to applying the life-changing truth we have learned.

When I take verses I learned as a child and give them new words, I capture a thought with freshness and put it into imagery that revives its impact on my mind and stirs my will to renewed action. For example, Proverbs 3:5-6 cannot be improved upon for directness, clarity, simplicity, and ease of recall when I need it (which is frequently). "Trust in the LORD with all thine heart; and lean not unto thine own understanding. In all thy ways acknowledge him and he shall direct thy paths" (KJV).

But the meaning is rejuvenated for me when I examine it and give it new words:

"Put your confidence 100 percent in the Lord—especially when things don't make sense. Don't rely on your own cleverness and imperfect human wisdom. Give Him the captain's wheel for every circumstance of life, and He will keep you on course through the wildest storm and the roughest, uncharted sea."

The first three methods we are studying in this course—four-questions, devotional, and paraphrase—form a kind of basic tool kit for all our future studies. The four-question method helps us gather information. Devotional studies guide us in application and worship. Paraphrasing is an exercise in summarizing and personalizing all we learn.

How shall we go about paraphrasing? Is it enough just to read the passage and write whatever thoughts come to us? No.

Paraphrasing is more complex than that. Before we begin, we need a bit of background to enable us to know what to think about what we read. All the methods you learn in this course will increase your fund of helpful knowledge upon which to base your understanding and application of truth. Paraphrasing will grow richer and more meaningful to you as you learn each new method.

At this point, however, it is wise to learn some things about the paraphrasing technique. Then you can develop the habit of paraphrasing the application of Bible truth, as a part of every study you do.

What kinds of background materials should you search for before you are ready to paraphrase?

First, *check the context.* Learn how the passage fits into the overall picture, and what its real meaning is.

Second, *use the basic four-question method to determine the meaning of the passage for you personally.* In doing that, you will discover a main theme. Perhaps you will build your paraphrase around the main theme. Or some minor theme may jump out at you from your reading and speak to you where you live or hurt or where you need to work on a weak spot. In that case, paraphrase the minor theme—whatever helps you to fit the passage to your needs and situation.

Third, a helpful technique for finding the message is to *compare all the translations you have available.* Different translators approach each passage from different angles. Often the total of their works will give you a composite picture of some complex truth that could never be fully translated by a single statement in our English language.

Fourth, when you encounter trouble with word meanings, *go to your concordance.* This valuable tool can give you the precise sense of the word. You will find a limited number of definitions in the margins of your Bible or handbooks. If you do not find what you need there, go on. Searching out the meanings of words you are not sure of is essential. Obscure non-images left in your mind by unsolved word-meaning puzzles can never meet your needs adequately.

Finally, *follow all the rules we have discussed in a previous lesson for interpreting Scripture.* If you come across a passage you cannot clear up with your most diligent study tactics, do not panic. You are probably not ready for it. Whatever kind of Bible study you approach, you are going to encounter some things you cannot handle. Knowing that such things are normal allows one to accept them in stride.

This is one place where Bible study differs from the study of other textbooks. Suppose you spend $50 to take a college course. Then you buy a textbook for $25. When you discover that parts of the textbook are beyond your comprehension and that you can never pass your $50 course until you are able to handle those mysterious passages, you will have reason to panic.

When you read your Bible and find things you cannot handle, set them aside for a time. No failing grade will appear on your report card because you did not absorb a specific passage in a given time period. You have a whole lifetime to study this textbook. If you never master certain portions, you can simply add them to the list of questions you plan to ask God in person when you get to heaven.

We need to remind ourselves that whenever we come to frustrations of any kind in Bible study, Satan taunts us and tries to make us feel like second class Christians because we have not yet learned some things. No matter how much we learn, he will always point to our ignorance and suggest, "Now isn't that discouraging?"

On the authority of Jesus Christ, we can rout him with a clear retort: "It is only discouraging if I listen to you; and that I never have to do!"

Once you have laid the foundations, found the backgrounds, and dug out all the meanings, how do you actually begin to write your paraphrase? What form do you use?

Because this exercise in worshipful study is such a personal thing, there are no limits to the ways you can handle it. You can choose from a wide variety of forms. No one can tell you exactly how to write your paraphrase. However, here are a few guidelines that will help you proceed:

1. *Make your paraphrase personal.* It should be a one-of-a-kind expression of your personality on paper. For several

years, I have collected paraphrases of 1 Corinthians 13, which illustrate this principle beautifully. Each is as unique as the person who wrote it. As I share a few short excerpts from different ones, see what they tell you about the person who wrote them.

> Even though I sound more interesting than Walter Cronkite or Barbara Walters and have not love, I am just a noisy commercial.   Shirley Wimmer

> If I can learn to write with the pen of a C. S. Lewis or the apostle Paul, but do not have love for my neighbor, I am nothing more than a talented showoff and an offensive prig.
>   Ethel Herr

> If I could throw my paper route blindfolded, but did not have love for each of my customers, I would be just as well off sitting in a closet the rest of my life.[1]   Greg Enos

> If I knew all about the rules of pedagogy, and were able to apply them to all learning situations and had not love, it would be useless.   Grace Hammer

As you write your paraphrase, you may not be terribly original. It does not matter whether you have any special gift for writing or whether you are clumsy on paper. Do not let that deter you. Just make it express you, because it is for only you and the Lord. No other human being need ever see it. Think of it as an act of Bible study and worship that you are offering to God so He can use it to effect growth in your life.

2. In your paraphrase *you may wish to stick closely to the text of the Scripture.* Here is one that does:

> Suppose I were able to preach with eloquence, and suppose I could even speak in tongues. If I did it without any love in my heart, my words would be as welcome as a chalk screeching on a blackboard or the blat of a diesel horn at midnight.   Robert Hill

---

1. Greg Enos, "1 Corinthians 13: A Paperboy's Paraphrase," *Moody Monthly,* September 1979.

The nuclear physicist who wrote that has followed the pattern of the passage with technical precision. Yet, he has illuminated it and made it touch us where we can feel and understand. The imagery is so realistic that it makes us cringe to read it.

3. *You can base your paraphrase on the main theme and not necessarily make it stick closely to the text.* I once took the Beatitudes and did them in reverse. Instead of saying, as Jesus did, that a woman is blessed for doing certain things, I examined why it is that if she does the opposite, she will have trouble. Here is one of them that describes the opposite of the poor in spirit who shall inherit the kingdom of God:

> She who has it all down here may grow cocky, dull, and unappreciative. What would heaven's kingdom do for her? Those streets of gold could never satisfy the cravings of a greedy soul. [from Matthew 5:3]

4. *You may concentrate on a minor theme out of the passage.* Here is one written by a high school girl on a basketball team. She took just a part of the passage (1 Corinthians 13) and emphasized a minor theme—the definition of love:

> Love is being able to smile when the referee makes a bad call. Chris Troolines

That paraphrase is practical, even to non-basketball-players. I do not have a referee in my kitchen, but I have other things and people who irritate me just as much. That paraphrase speaks clearly to me in my kitchen, even though it is written about basketball courts.

5. *You may take a single line of Scripture and let your mind freely expand on all that it involves in practical daily application to your life.* For example, from the line "So will you be filled through all your being with God Himself" (Ephesians 3:19, Phillips), I wrote this expanded paraphrase:

> May you turn again and again to Him in worship. May you learn to think like God—to see all of life from His point of view.

May you know the surpassing and exquisite joy of sharing everything in your life and circumstances and consciousness with Him.

I went on for a whole page with those thoughts and could have done more. This type of paraphrase is rarely ever ended.

6. Finally, *there are many other personalized forms to choose from.* You may rewrite a whole chapter or a prayer that expresses your reaction to the passage. Here is one that came to me when I was considering Matthew 6:33 ("Seek ye first the kingdom of God and his righteousness and all these things shall be added unto you," KJV):

> Forgive me, Father
> for seeking first
> the preservation
> of my comforts
> while praying
> that the furtherance
> of Your kingdom
> will be added
> unto You.

You may write a poetic summary of the theme, as in this one from Hebrews 11, the Faith chapter of the Bible. It is a short, pithy reminder of an eternal truth so often lost in the ugliness of daily living:

> Abraham
>   Isaac
> Joseph
>   Moses
> sought a part of
> God's kingdom to be.
> Have faith!
> Be sure of things
> you hope for,
> certain of things
> you cannot see.

Beth Riddle

With those guidelines as a background, let us look at an exercise in paraphrasing the familiar chapter, 1 Corinthians 13. We are going to look at the overall theme of the chapter and then zero in on verse 7 for our actual paraphrase sample.

First, consider the *context*. This classic passage on God's love in human expression deals with the subject in such depth that we would expect it to have been written to a mature, loving church. If we back up and start reading at 1 Corinthians 1, however, we discover that Paul was sharing this literary and spiritual masterpiece with a lukewarm, immature church that had serious moral problems and was torn by fierce competition.

Among other things, those Christians were concerned about having the best, most impressive spiritual gifts. Hence, they were hung up on external things, when God wanted them to concentrate on getting their hearts right with Him. They all wanted the showy gifts so they could show off how spiritual they were. No one seemed interested in a simple gift of humble ministry operating behind the scenes for the eyes and glory of God alone.

To counter that shallow thinking, Paul tells them in chapter 12 what the gifts of the Spirit are, where they come from, and what their purpose is. In chapter 14, he tells them about proper and improper uses of some of the more showy gifts such as tongues. Sandwiched between those two instructional chapters, we find this little gem—1 Corinthians 13. Knowing the proper placement of the chapter helps us fully to grasp its message. We now see it as a picture of God's ideal gift, open to all His children, standing in marked contrast to the other individual gifts that those carnally minded people were fighting over.

Second, what is the *theme?* Love, of course, is the broad theme. But when we get more specific, we find this message: God's kind of love affects every area of human life and is the greatest possible spiritual gift.

Third, we can *compare other translations* and find a lot of interesting things. There are many points of fascinating learning in this chapter. We shall simply look at verse 7. In the

King James Version, love "beareth all things." When we check other translations to get an accurate word meaning, we find the following:

"knows how to be silent" (Weymouth)

"always slow to expose" (Moffatt)

"never gives up" *(Today's English Version)*

"covers up everything" (Berkeley)

"excuses all things" (Riverside)

"knows no limits to its endurance" (Phillips)

"If you love someone you will always be loyal to him" *(The Living Bible)*.

With so many different ideas, it looks confusing at first. What is the connection between them all?

In most cases such comparison will enrich our understanding of a word. This time, we will need to go on to the next step in order to arrive at a clear meaning.

Fourth, turn to a *concordance* to find the meaning of the Greek word translated so variously. When we check out the word "beareth" in the concordance, we make a truly exciting discovery that brings all the translations together. But more, it opens up a beautiful picture of God's practical truth about love in action.

Literally, the word means "to roof over." Figuratively, it can be interpreted as "to cover with silence" or "to endure patiently" or "to excuse faults." The picture it paints is one of my brother with a deep problem that arises from his weakness. He needs protection from criticism and despair as he works his way through to victory and Christian maturity. God's love will enable me to build a roof over him. That means I will be silent, neither spreading news of his weakness nor browbeating him with "deserved lectures." I will be slow to expose his faults. When he does not measure up as fast as I think he should, I will not give up on him. I cover up everything and excuse him. There is no limit to my endurance, and I will always remain loyal to him, even when others pick him to pieces. I will strive to keep the roof intact over his head and help others to understand why he needs such a protective covering.

Finally, with that understanding clearly in mind, as with pain I remember the many people who have needed roofs and I let them down or let holes grow in their roofs, I am ready to *write my paraphrase.* In this case, it will be in the form of a confession.

"Dear Lord, forgive me for approaching my brothers and sisters with my limited store of human love—self-seeking, short-tempered, intolerant love. I now recognize that I have no excuses for not allowing You to offer Your indestructible, limitless, selfless love to them all through me. I also remember how wide and sturdy is the roof You maintain over my weaknesses. Lord, make me a builder and patcher of roofs."

One word of caution. Be careful that some phrase does not trigger a theological concept you are particularly anxious to defend. Ask God to keep you objective, to stop you from reading into each verse an apologetic for your pet doctrine.

Paraphrasing Scripture is designed to help us better grasp its meaning and apply it. So we must come to God's Word with open minds. If you find a phrase that you know so well that you are certain you know precisely what it is all about, examine it with special care. You are bringing to that passage far too many preconceived ideas. Ask God to challenge your thinking and open your horizons to the vast possibilities that lie beyond your present learning and understanding.

ASSIGNMENT:

1. Paraphrase Matthew 6:9-13 (Lord's Prayer). Jesus gave this prayer to His disciples as a pattern of the ingredients of mature praying. It was His open invitation to personal paraphrasing.
2. Add to the list of further Bible Study Ideas at the end of lesson 1 your ideas for other paraphrases.

PARAPHRASE WORKSHEET

SCRIPTURE PASSAGE:

BACKGROUND: (context)

Who wrote this?
To whom?
Why?

THEME OF THE PASSAGE:

THEME YOU WANT TO EMPHASIZE:

TRANSLATION COMPARISONS:

CONCORDANCE WORD MEANINGS:

PARAPHRASE: (Use more paper if needed.)

LESSON 7
Studying a Story

What happens when you read a familiar Bible story? Do you read only half the words, skimming the rest because you know it so well?

Do you try to place yourself in the shoes of the characters and imagine what they must have felt and how they grew through the experience?

Do you get excited about it as a beloved story that seems to get better with each reading?

Do you read with extra care, always searching for something you may have missed on previous readings?

Bible stories are potent sources of either unparalleled learning or absolute boredom. If we do not know how to study them, they can become dull and tarnished with familiarity and overexposure on the surface level. Or we can carry false impressions of details that we picked up the first time we heard the story. We may misapply the lessons we think they are trying to teach. Worst of all, we can ignore them because we feel no great need for them. In the process, we rob ourselves of some of God's deepest treasures of divine truth.

On the other hand, once we learn how to approach them, Bible stories can enrich our lives and give us a balanced perspective on all God's truth. Knowing how to study Bible sto-

ries is one of the essential foundation stones for other kinds of
Bible studies. Major portions of the Bible appear in story form.
We cannot expect to grasp the full teaching of Scripture on
any topic without learning how to read, interpret, and apply
the truths contained in Bible stories.

In order to learn some effective ways to handle these spiritual and literary gems, in this lesson we want to answer three
questions.

Why did God choose to reveal so much truth in story form?

First, God has so structured us that we love stories. The ancient Jewish rabbis said, "God made man because He loves
stories."[1] Our love for stories is a part of being made in the
image of God. God built into us the love for stories, then
communicated His truth to us in that form.

Second, stories embody truth. Bible stories never tell us
anything simply to entertain. Although some are entertaining,
their primary function is to illustrate truth. They do it by putting flesh and bones and personality on the facts and making
them live.

There is sometimes a summary statement of truth at either
the beginning or end of a story, but the message is clear from
reading the story itself. Biblical writers put flesh and blood
and heart and mind into real people in real circumstances and
real places, and thus they embody truth in a way that we can
understand.

In Luke 10:25-37, a contentious young lawyer posed a theological question to Jesus in the hope of avoiding the practical
implications of God's truth. Jesus had reminded the man that
the commandments of the Law, which he so rigidly upheld,
could be summarized in one two-pronged statement: "You
shall love the LORD your God with all your heart, and with all
your soul and with all your strength and with all your mind;
and your neighbor as yourself" (v. 27).

Attempting to skirt the issue, the lawyer answered, "And
who is my neighbor?"

---

1. Leland Ryken, "The Bible: God's Storybook," *Christianity Today,* 5 Octo-
    ber 1979, p. 34.

Jesus could have turned to him and delivered a logical, three-point sermon that would have covered the topic more than adequately. He could have given him a long list of the kinds of people that were his neighbors.

Instead, He told a story—the parable of the Good Samaritan. Filled with painfully familiar imagery, the story pointed directly to the heart of the message and touched the young man where he could not squirm out of the trap he had inadvertently set for himself. Over and over, Jesus used that technique in His teaching ministry, for He knew that a good story embodies truth.

Third, a story allows us to experience truth. When God wanted to tell us that the most important thing we ever do is spend time with Him, worshiping and listening to His truth, He did not issue a statement or preach a sermon. Once more, He shared a story—this time of Mary and Martha. Read it in Luke 10:38-42.

As you read that story, you can visualize the whole thing. You see the neat little house, smell the food cooking in the kitchen, feel the tensions, hear Jesus' soothing words and Martha's irritated voice. You identify with one or more of the characters, feel the startled shock of the impact of Jesus' answer. In your imagination, you may even become one of the characters. Suddenly you are able to apply the truth to your own busy life where the daily grind of duties seems so important. You recognize the need to put it all in perspective by taking time for God, who longs for your companionship more than anything else.

Finally, a story shows us most convincingly that God is active in the affairs of men. We rarely see a story in the Bible where God is not the main character. Even where His name is not mentioned, He is always there as a backdrop. The rightness and wrongness of the actions of the human characters is continually brought into focus by the God who is pictured as the Creator of moral law. God never appears or speaks in the story of the Good Samaritan, but we sense His presence in the deep levels of the story. The priest, Levite, and robbers have broken His laws. The Good Samaritan lives by them and is presented as our fine example.

What makes a story a story? During the sixties and seventies a lot of counter-culture people insisted that a story does not have to say anything or go anywhere. It could simply ramble on without direction or point, letting the writer pour out his heart on the blank pages with no need for structure or identity. That notion often represented the thinking of confused persons whose lives were unresolved. To them, life was a continuous series of haphazard happenstances with no cement to hold it together. Such ramblings are not stories. God has built into the human heart the need to resolve things. A genuine story must have a pattern of some sort and a resolution.

In other words, a story needs a plot based on strong conflict. The sequence of events must be built around a problem and developed progressively toward a solution.

As previously noted, the Scripture has one master plot. In addition, each story has its own individual plot, with an immediate problem or conflict to be solved. Characters interact with God, each other, or Satan. Major portions of the Bible are devoted to dialogue that reveals personality and character and moves the story along. All those techniques draw us into the scene and enable us to see, hear, and feel the tensions and fellowship between characters.

In the story of Mary and Martha, we see an excellent example of two kinds of conflict found in all Bible stories. First, the surface conflict, the obvious problem shown in a confrontation between the three characters. In this sisters' quarrel, Mary wants to visit with Jesus, while Martha is irritated that she is not busy with her as she fusses about the kitchen making elaborate preparations for the meal.

As we look closely at the story, though, we see the deep conflict. It is a conflict of priorities, between practical, work-oriented Martha and Jesus (the God-character). In every Bible story, look beneath the surface for the deep conflict. The key to finding it is to ask, Where is God in this story? What is the conflict between Him and the human characters?

Another element of plot is choice. Whether there is open conflict or not, there have to be choices. As we study Bible stories, we learn that man is what he is, he lives as he lives, and he receives either blessings or judgments—all based on his choices. In our story, Martha chose to ask Jesus to put pressure on her sister to assist her. Jesus chose to point to Martha's blind spot and take advantage of that teachable moment. Mary chose to sit at Jesus' feet.

A story needs, as a part of the plot, a clearly discernible beginning, middle, and ending. That sounds simple. Of course a story begins, continues, and finishes, but it must do so according to a plan. The beginning introduces what is going on, the middle shows the plot progressing, and the ending wraps the story up in a satisfying conclusion. Good storytelling demands planning and care of a type that is always demonstrated in the stories of the Bible.

The Luke 10 story begins (v. 38) with a time setting ("as they were traveling along"), character introductions, a place setting ("a certain village"), and an occasion ("Martha welcomed Him into her home"). The story continues (vv. 39-40) in progressive order, building to a point of climax, where Martha confronts Jesus with her poignant question. Finally, Jesus concludes the story (vv. 41-42) with His satisfying answer and thus reveals both the deep conflict and the divine solution.

One thing you may notice as you read Bible stories is that certain details are omitted. For example, why does Luke 10:38 say "a certain village" instead of naming the place? Were the two sisters unmarried? Was there a man living in the house? How wealthy were they? Did Jesus stop there often?

As with all storytelling, the author chose only those details that were needed to present the theme (which, you remember, is the reason for telling this story in the first place). You can often find further information in one of four ways. First, you may find the details by searching deeper into the story and asking questions. The financial status of Martha and Mary may be evidenced by the fact that Martha did not call on her household servants to prepare and serve the meal.

Second, sometimes you can check other Scripture references for details. In so doing, we learn that Martha and Mary lived with their brother, Lazarus (John 11:1-2), who was a close friend of Jesus' (John 11). We discover that they lived in Bethany (John 11:1), where Jesus visited on other occasions as well (Matthew 21:17).

Third, search your handbook, encyclopedia, atlas, and the like for some details. An atlas tells us that Bethany was located about two miles from Jerusalem. That helps us to understand that Jesus could have visited there often, when He was teaching in Jerusalem.

Fourth, if the details are unavailable, they are not important to either the plot or the theme. That is what we must assume about the Scripture's silence on the marital status of every member of this family.

Besides conflict, choice, and structure, stories need to show us real characters acting like real people in real circumstances. They show us clearly what the characters' personalities are like, how they feel, what motivates them, and how they react to people, circumstances, and God. Bible characters are real. Further, they are presented in relation to God and to His perfect standards of holiness, might, and justice.

Martha and Mary are real, believable people—the kind we can identify with. They live in a real home in a historically documented village. They extend hospitality, prepare meals, visit with their guests, scold one another, try to manipulate each other through Jesus' influence. Even Jesus is a real person. Not only was He the great Teacher in this story; He also needed a bed, a meal, and some fellowship. Martha was irritable, Mary was dreamy and maybe lazy.

Finally, stories need, with all their realism, to offer us some hope in life. Jesus lifted all the realism of Luke 10:38-42 to a level of hope by His words of commendation to Mary. In effect, He was saying; "When we put these domestic conflicts in divine perspective, there is something for us all to learn."

Realism without hope creates depression. God never does that to us. Because He is a God of healing, restoration, and growth, He always provides a way through Himself to avoid judgment and destruction. Look for the combination of realism and hope in all the stories of the Bible. You will not be disappointed.

How can we get all the juice out of a story? First, if you are literarily inclined, you can do a literary analysis of the story. That is what we have just done with the Luke 10 account. A Literary Analysis Worksheet is provided for you at the end of this chapter. It is not essential; however, I include it here for those adventurous souls whose literary muscles itch for exercise.

What you all can do is follow the Four-Question Method, using the enclosed Bible Story Worksheet, which we will now cover in sample form, again using the now-familiar story of Luke 10:38-42.

As in previous sample lessons, instructions are enclosed in parentheses. Sample entry materials are italicized.

I. WHAT DO I SEE:

WHO? (List all the people mentioned in the story)

Jesus and His disciples, Martha, Mary

WHERE?

In Martha's home in a certain village

WHEN?

As Jesus and His disciples were traveling

WHAT HAPPENED? (It may seem elementary to list the sequence of events in a familiar story. Do it anyway. That enables you to get a fresh view and correct any errors that may be ingrained in your thinking.)

1. *Jesus stopped to visit, at Martha's invitation.*
2. *Mary sat to listen to Jesus' words.*
3. *Martha made elaborate meal preparations.*
4. *Martha complained about Mary's lack of helpfulness.*
5. *Jesus rebuked Martha and defended Mary's actions.*

WHAT ATTITUDES ARE DEMONSTRATED?

Mary—preoccupation with Jesus and love for Him
Martha—desire to please, irritability, judgmentalism
Jesus—calm authority, eagerness to communicate divine truth

WHAT CUSTOMS OF THE DAY DO I NEED TO LEARN ABOUT?

Sitting at Jesus' feet to learn (v. 39)

KEY WORDS OR PHRASES: (Choose words that seem important to understanding anything about the story.)

Distracted (v. 40), worried, and bothered (v. 41)

II. WHAT DOES IT MEAN?

WHY THESE PEOPLE? (Compare the account with other references to these people. Learn all you can about them.)

Jesus—guest of honor, good friend, the God-character
Martha—hostess, possibly owner of the home
Mary—sister whose unorthodox behavior triggered a teachable moment

WHY THIS PLACE?

From John 11:1, 18 we learn that it was Bethany, near Jerusalem. Likely it was a common stopover spot in many of Jesus' travels.

WHY AT THIS TIME?

He needed a place to stay on His journey.

WHY THESE EVENTS? (Ask the "why" of each of the numbered events in sequence under "What happened?")

1. *Jesus was tired and needed refreshing.*
2. *Mary longed to learn of Jesus.*
3. *Martha wanted to please Jesus by fixing a fine meal.*
4. *Martha could not understand that Mary chose to please Jesus by listening to Him. It was not Martha's way to visit as long as He was unfed.*
5. *Jesus wanted to teach both women a lesson in priorities.*

WHY THESE ATTITUDES? (Again, refer to each attitude listed in the previous section.)

Mary's preoccupation—love for Jesus, spiritual hunger. Mar-

*tha's irritability and judgmentalism—confused motives.
More concerned about adhering to custom and making impression than about learning and building relationship with
Jesus. Jesus' calm authority—He was God and had the final
word.*

<u>WHY THESE CUSTOMS?</u> (Look for answers to questions
about customs you do not understand in handbooks, encyclopedias, dictionaries, etc.)

*Sitting at Jesus' feet to learn. Guests often sat on the floor in
Israelite homes of Jesus' day. Further, it was most unusual for
a woman to sit in company with the men of the house when
they were in conversation. Since Jesus was traveling with His
disciples and since, as we know from John 11:1-2, these wom-
en had a brother, we can assume that other men were present
at this time.*

<u>WHY THESE KEY WORDS?</u> (Use concordance to find
meanings. Note how these words and phrases are used elsewhere in the Bible.)

Distracted—distracted with care
Worried—anxious about
Bothered—disturbed

III. <u>WHAT DOES THIS MEAN TO ME?</u>

<u>PROMISES TO CLAIM:</u> (Not all promises given in every sto-
ry are meant for us to claim in our quite different times and
circumstances. We must compare them with what we already
know of the Scriptures and look carefully at our circumstances
before we claim them.)

*Jesus promised that the "better part" would not be taken from
Mary. We can claim this within reason. However, it is no
blanket excuse for us to avoid work that needs to be done and
spend all day everyday reading the Bible and praying. Compare Isaiah 1:10-20 and Mark 7:10-13, where the principle is
clear that religious exercise never excuses us from family
responsibilities.*

<u>COMMANDS TO OBEY:</u> (In stories, commands are rarely
given to us directly. Usually we find God instructing His people to follow some divine principle He is trying to teach by

the story. Also, note that commands and promises are closely connected. Most of God's promises are conditional—You trust and obey, and I will reward your faith and action.)

The only command in our story is an implied one—Do not force Mary to give up the superior thing she has chosen.

EXAMPLES TO FOLLOW OR AVOID:

Follow:

Martha's willing hospitality

Mary's devotion to learning from Jesus

Jesus' wisdom in handling domestic conflicts with godly counseling

Avoid:

Martha's overanxiety with elaborate hospitality

Martha's judgmental attitude based on lack of understanding.

IV. HOW WILL MY LIFE BE DIFFERENT AFTER STUDYING THIS STORY?

1. *I will extend hospitality willingly.*
2. *I will strive for a balance between caring for people's physical needs and ministering to their spiritual needs.*
3. *I will strive for a balance between work and worship.*
4. *I will ask God to give me a heart that understands my brothers and sisters with different temperaments, attitudes, and ways of handling situations.*

(As you have gone through this story with me, perhaps you found things I missed. That is part of the excitement of Bible study—it is inexhaustible. After doing this lesson, you may find it helpful to study John 11 as well.)

ASSIGNMENT:

1. Study the story of Jesus' first miracle in John 2:1-11, using the Bible Story Worksheet.

2. Record on the Future Ideas Worksheet at the end of lesson 1 any other story study ideas that come to you.

BIBLE STUDY WORKSHEET

I. WHAT DO I SEE?

WHO?

WHERE?

WHAT HAPPENED?

WHAT ATTITUDES ARE DEMONSTRATED?

WHAT CUSTOMS DO I NEED TO LEARN ABOUT?

WHAT KEY WORDS AND PHRASES ARE HERE?

II. WHAT DOES IT MEAN?

WHY THESE PEOPLE?

WHY THIS PLACE?

WHY AT THIS TIME?

WHY THESE EVENTS?

WHY THESE ATTITUDES?

WHY THESE CUSTOMS?

WHY THESE KEY WORDS AND PHRASES?

III. WHAT DOES IT MEAN TO ME?

PROMISES TO CLAIM?

COMMANDS TO OBEY?

EXAMPLES TO FOLLOW OR AVOID?

IV. HOW WILL MY LIFE BE
DIFFERENT AFTER STUDYING
THIS STORY?

LITERARY ANALYSIS WORKSHEET

CONFLICTS:
      Surface:

      Deep

CHOICES:

STRUCTURE:

      Beginning

      Middle

      Ending

UNITY—MAIN THEME:

REALISTIC PICTURES AND EXPERIENCES:

EVIDENCE OF HOPE:

SUGGESTED BIBLE STORIES

This list is only a small starter list to help you begin:
Creation—Genesis 1
First murder—Genesis 4:1-15
Call of Abraham—Genesis 12:1-9
Birth of Moses—Exodus 2:1-10
Rahab and the scarlet cord—Joshua 2

David anointed king—1 Samuel 16:1-13
Elijah fed by a widow—1 Kings 17:1-16
Elisha and the multiplied oil—2 Kings 4:1-7
Daniel in lion's den—Daniel 6
Jesus' birth predicted—Luke 1:26-38
Baptism of Jesus—Matthew 3
Jesus' temptation—Matthew 4:1-11
Jesus calms the tempest—Mark 4:35-41
Jesus heals woman with issue of blood—Luke 8:43-48
Feeding of the five thousand—John 6:1-15
Healing ten lepers—Luke 17:11-19
Water into wine—John 2:1-11
Raising of Lazarus—John 11
Triumphal entry of Jesus—Mark 11:1-11
Last Supper—Mark 14:12-26
Jesus in Gethsemane—Matthew 26:36-46
Crucifixion—Luke 23:26-49
Peter's denial—John 18:15-18, 25-27
Resurrection—Matthew 28:1-10
Saul's conversion—Acts 9:1-22

LESSON 8
Studying a Prayer

On one occasion, as Jesus journeyed with His disciples, they found Him at prayer. When he had finished, one of the men voiced the feelings of the group.

"Lord, teach us to pray."

Do you ever feel that way? If so, do not hesitate to share that longing with God. Not only inexperienced baby Christians sense a strong need to learn about prayer. The more mature we become and the more we pray, the more we realize we have yet to learn about prayer. In this lesson, we are going to experiment with an effective method for sharpening our praying skills.

In the last lesson, we discovered that when we study Bible stories, we learn how God acts and expects us to act. Now we will discover that when we study Bible prayers, we learn what prayer is and how we ought to pray.

We all know something about prayer. We have heard it defined a dozen ways. We have listened to sermons and read books and articles about prayer. But when we examine the prayers of the people in Scripture, we uncover some of the most fascinating and vital dimensions of the whole subject.

When we study Bible prayers, we eavesdrop on saints of another time and place. Many of their prayers are imperfectly motivated, uneloquently expressed, loaded with complaints and pessimistic outbursts from fearful and trembling hearts. At times we are surprised to hear what sounds like ourselves praying in these passages. We note some painfully familiar selfish attitudes, small petitions, lack of faith, and surface-level requests. Most often though, we find gorgeous examples of deep praying that stir our hearts to attempt the same.

Most important, when we study Bible prayers, we learn what prayer is all about from God's point of view. Prayer is God's idea, not man's. He longs for our prayers. Those of us who are parents can understand that in a limited way. We have an urgent need for our children to communicate with us. We appreciate all the active ways they share their love—the washed dishes, the obedient actions, the Mother's Day cards. None of those, however, takes the place of spoken words. If a child never said with his lips, "I love you," or, "I need something," or, "Just wait until I tell you what happened today," the relationship would be far from satisfying. Similarly, God has invested His Father's heart heavily in us and can never be satisfied until we communicate with Him.

As we examine the prayers recorded for our learning in the Bible, we realize that prayer can be defined as *the response of the human spirit to a God who desires and takes the initiative in establishing a relationship of intimate fellowship with us, His unique creatures.* Always He is to be the center of our praying. Our needs are important. Often, they drive us to our knees when we would never make the time to go there otherwise. God wants us to bring our needs to Him, but they are never to be the center of our praying. We see that over and over in the lives of the Bible's praying saints. Even when people came to Him in tremendous need, God was still the center and the focus of their attention as they prayed.

Psalm 62:8 paints a vivid picture of the nature of prayer: "Trust Him at all times . . . pour out your heart before Him." That tells us that praying is not just reciting the Lord's Prayer at night before we fall asleep. It is not saying whatever comes off the top of our heads. Nor is it automatically rattling off names on a prayer list of persons we feel duty-bound to pray for. Rather, praying is pouring out our hearts to God. When we pour our something, we take off the cap and turn it upside down so that everything inside can spill out. That is what biblical prayer is—removing the cap and letting God have free access to all that our hearts contain. Note, though, that He is both our reason for doing that and the sole recipient of all the pouring-out action. We pour it out to Him because we "trust Him at all times."

Bible characters are like us in that they prayed for many different reasons. Their prayers were a total response of their total being to God. Many strong prayers arose out of urgent need. We all pray that way at times. Such prayers are rarely well thought out, well phrased, or profoundly expressed. They are simply a bursting forth of the compressed contents of troubled hearts.

Most Bible prayers are personal, but not all. Many arise from deep burdens carried for the needs of others. We can identify with that as well. We love our friends and feel constrained to pray for their desperate needs. Often their needs prompt more of this type of praying than our own needs do, because we tend to feel that we can handle our own problems ourselves. When it is somebody else, we do not fully understand the issues and cannot do the job for them. We are shut up to prayer.

Sometimes Bible prayers were not connected with urgent needs at all. *Some came as responses to God's words.* They differed, depending on the revelation of God that prompted them. At times God spoke and devastated the person with conviction; that brought him to his knees in confession. At other times, he was led to worship, praise, and adoration of God for His wisdom, providential love, and the like. Sometimes the child of God brought Him his questions. Studying Bible prayers teaches us that when we bring to God our questions of wisdom, specific guidance, or theological puzzles, the answer does not always come immediately. We are not always ready to receive answers to the things that mystify and confuse us. If we are persistent, in time, we will know what He expects of us.

Bible prayers were sometimes responses to God's actions. Again, we can identify with that. Who of us has not at some time been completely overwhelmed when God did something for us in answer to prayer or even before we had asked?

I had prayed for one friend's spiritual healing for over ten years. Many times I begged God to let me give up. He simply said, "Pray without ceasing!" Then the miracles began to happen. God got through to her, and she responded. The growth of faith came slowly with many setbacks and hindrances along the way. Today, though, that woman is rejoicing in what great things God has done for her. Often I pray a simple prayer of response to His mighty acts in her hopeless life, "Lord, You are great! Thank You for accomplishing the impossible!"

In the Bible, I read of others who experienced that same kind of thing and responded in worship and praise. As a result, my faith is strengthened to go on praying for other impossibilities.

As we study Bible prayers, we observe that there are several different elements of prayer—the various components that make up the all-encompassing picture. First, we find two similar elements that are often thought to be identical—*praise* and *thanksgiving. Praise* thanks God for who He is—His character, His person, His love, His perfection, and His purity. *Thanksgiving* thanks Him for what He does.

At times, we do not feel very thankful for what God is doing, because it hurts. Even then, we can praise Him for who He is, if we have learned that He loves us far too much to give us anything but the best. When He has allowed us to lose a loved one, our material possessions, or our health, we can still praise Him for who He is—our wise and loving Father. We find the precedent for this kind of praying in Job's story. When he had lost his children and his wealth, he "fell to the ground and worshiped. And he said . . . The LORD gave and the LORD has taken away. Blessed be the name of the LORD" (Job 1:20-21). Later, when he had lost his health and the goodwill of his friends, he said, "Though He slay me, I will hope in Him" (13:15).

A third element of prayer is *worship*. Worship grows out of praise. It is the total, open, unreserved response of my being to God Himself. Often, I cannot put it into words. Worship may consist of a silent communication in which the heart and mind are completely absorbed in an overwhelming awe of God. Sometimes as I read the Psalms, I get the feeling that the psalmist ran out of adequate words to express the deep worship of his heart.

"O LORD our Lord, how excellent is thy name in all the earth!" (Psalm 8:1, KJV).

"As the hart panteth after the water brooks, so panteth my soul after thee, O God. My soul thirsteth for God" (Psalm 42:1-2, KJV).

"Great is the LORD, and greatly to be praised" (Psalm 48:1, KJV).

That is worship!

A fourth element is *petition*, which is asking God to meet my own personal needs. The fifth is closely related to it—*intercession*, which is praying for the needs of others. Those are the two most used elements of praying. In fact some people think that is all prayer is. Studying Bible prayers shows us that there is more. It also shows us what kinds of requests are right and proper and how to make them effective. Finally, it shows us the importance of all the other elements in preparing us to make our requests.

The sixth element of prayer is what we call *complaint* or *lament*. We do not necessarily mean this in the sense of blaming God for mistreating us. We refer here to the all-inclusive outpouring of our hearts when we are upset. My son called me on the telephone one day to tell me of a disturbing thing that had happened with his landlord. It was going to prove costly to him, and he was upset. When I assured him that though I could not do anything about it, I would pray, he said, "That's OK. I only needed somebody to yell at."

Often when life gets too much for us and we need somebody to yell at, God is there. He listens patiently until we are through. Then, He may give us an instant answer, or we may have found our own answer in the unburdening process. Or He may ask us to wait awhile or go on struggling with the problem. In any case, He is the ultimate source of comfort for all of us when we hurt. Prayers in the Bible show us many examples of this kind of praying. They provide us with guidelines for keeping complaint from turning into accusation and confidence in God from turning into bitterness.

Finally, we have two more companion elements—*confession* and *commitment.* They are the elements we so easily forget, neglect, or consciously sidestep. Requests and complaints are easy to include. Occasionally we remember to give thanks, praise, or even worship. When it comes to confession or commitment, our human natures back off because those elements are costly.

Confession says, "OK, Lord, I understand your viewpoint on what I have done or thought or where my motivations were not worthy of You. I accept Your verdict and admit that I grieved Your heart."

Commitment goes one step further and adds, "Because of what You have said to me in Your Word and on my knees, I am ready now to make an about-face, to go in the direction You have pointed out for me." As we study Bible prayers, we see that such commitments are dangerous if our hearts are not in them. God holds us accountable for every word we speak, even in prayer.

So that we can learn to study Bible prayers and learn from them the specific lessons God wants to teach us, we have included two things in this lesson. First is a list of Bible prayers you can study. They are grouped into fifteen different categories. In some cases a prayer might fit into more than one category, but I have included it in the one that I believe is its basic classification. The list is nowhere near exhaustive. It is simply designed to give you a start.

Second, I have provided a prayer study worksheet that outlines a progressive, step-by-step approach to prayer studies. In order to help you understand how to use the worksheet, we will look at Psalm 51 for our sample study.

Instructions are enclosed in parentheses. Sample entry materials are italicized.

SCRIPTURE PASSAGE: (Read it through at least once.)
   Psalm 51

BACKGROUND MATERIAL: (Find out, if possible, what gave rise to this prayer. If you have a marginal reference in your Bible, it will refer you to 2 Samuel 11-12. If not, in this case there is an explanatory note beneath the psalm number that tells you "A Psalm of David, when Nathan the prophet came unto him, after he had gone in to Bathsheba." That gives you a clue to take the word "Bathsheba" to your concordance and find where her story is located. Many of the psalms—which are the richest concentration of Bible prayers—do not give you any indication of their background. Wherever they do, however, search them out. Most other prayers are found in sequential context. When reading background materials, look for the following things.)

Time and place: (Locate events on your Bible Time Line Chart and on a map. Find out who was in control of the government and what great political power ruled the world.)

This occurred in the early days of the yet-undivided Kingdom of Israel, while David was king. It happened in Jerusalem.

Customs: (Identify and study to understand any customs that may be different from ours today. In addition, ask yourself, How much did people know about God at the time this prayer was offered? Try to restrict your thinking to the things that would be known or understood by the person offering the prayer you are studying.)

Polygamy was still accepted by society, at least for kings and rulers. David knew God as the author of a demanding moral and ceremonial law. He knew he had broken the moral law and that sacrifices were demanded for such sins. Little had ever been said, however, about confession and begging for forgiveness.

(Look for meanings of other customs such as the time of

year when kings went to battle, bathing customs that made this situation possible, and others you may find here.)

Sequence of events that led to the prayer:

David stayed home from battle. He saw Bathsheba, was tempted, took her to bed. When she became pregnant, he called his servant to see to it that her husband was killed in battle. Once Uriah was dead, David took Bathsheba to be his wife. Nathan the prophet of God finally had to come and accuse David of his sin.

Person offering the prayer: (What do you know about him from other accounts? Often previous stories about the characters will open doors and windows into their personalities and relationship with God that make the prayer more understandable.)

David's actions in 2 Samuel 11 and 12 seem out of character for this man who was called by God "a man after mine own heart" (Acts 13:22, KJV). But the depth of his character and true godliness show through when Nathan points the finger at him and he reacts. He could have denied the charges, justified himself, blamed somebody else, had Nathan executed—anything but confess and make restitution. Only a true man of God would do what he did—confess his wrongdoing and plead with God for forgiveness.

(When examining a character, ask yourself, How would I have reacted in a similar circumstance? It is amazing how such a question, if we face it honestly and realistically, will help us to see the genuine depth of our subject's character.)

REPEATED WORDS AND PHRASES: (As with all kinds of Bible study, these are keys to the theme or focus of the prayer.)

In Psalm 51, most repeated words are "Thy" and "Thou." Thy lovingkindness, Thy compassion, Thy righteousness, Thy praise, Thou dost speak. Eleven times David says "Thy" and four times "Thou." That tells us that God is the center and focus of the prayer. His confession is no guilt trip filled with self-pity for being so rotten. David admits his guilt, then concentrates on the holiness and goodness of God wherein lie his hope for restoration.

Other repeated ideas are significant—wash, cleanse, purify, restore, deliver, blot out my iniquities, and so on.

NAMES GIVEN TO GOD: (God reveals Himself to people by certain names in order to tell them something about Himself. People address God by some specific name as a revelation of how they feel about God. Looking at the names used by the man or woman at prayer helps us get inside that man or woman.)

David was a master at using a variety of descriptive names for God. Here, in his time of contrition, he used four simple names—God, God of my salvation, Lord, and Holy Spirit. Four times his broken heart burst out with "O God!" Broken hearts rarely spawn eloquence. David had been reduced to the knowledge that He had offended God and he could not even lift his head, much less come up with creative names for God.

THEME OF THE PRAYER: (Based on all your knowledge of circumstances, repeated phrases, names for God, and character of the one praying, you are ready to summarize, in a one-sentence capsulized thought, one basic thing this person was trying to say to God.)

David was saying, "O God, I confess my inexcusable sin and plead for restoration to fellowship with You." If he had been like many of us, he would have been content to be cleared of guilt and go on his way with a clean conscience. Not David. He insisted on being restored to his former place of fellowship and intimacy with God. That tells us that David was first and above all a lover of his God.

ELEMENTS OF PRAYER INCLUDED: (Very few prayers will contain all the elements. Most will contain more than one. Note, too, the order in which the elements occur.)

Confession (vv. 1-4); Petition (vv. 5-14); Praise (vv. 14-15); Worship (vv. 16-19).

The order teaches us that when there is sin, confession must come first, or all else will be useless. Prayer is reserved for persons in fellowship with God or persons who desire that fellowship above all else in life.

<u>LESSONS FOR MY PRAYER LIFE:</u> (I found at least six lessons in this passage, but I have listed for you only three of them.)

Cleansing is needed for fellowship with God.

Cleansing comes only through contrition and confession.

I must be totally honest with God when I approach Him.

<u>PARAPHRASE:</u> (Write a paraphrase that will help you to remember what you have learned and clinch the commitment you have made from this study.)

Lord, Your plan is for me to be totally honest about my feelings and motivations—honest enough to face the truth about my relationships with people and with You. You want me to allow Your truth to cut through my comfortable sufficiency and self-righteousness to the innermost control center of my being. Then alone will You be free to flood my whole life with Your absolutely dazzling light and give me a truly effective ministry to others in need (based on v. 6).

Assignment:

1. Using the following worksheet, study the prayer found in Psalm 57.

2. Record in the Future Ideas Worksheet at the end of lesson 1 any ideas you find for other prayer studies.

Biblical Prayers

<u>Thanksgiving</u>

Moses—Exodus 15

Deborah—Judges 5

David—2 Samuel 22; Psalm 18

Hannah—1 Samuel 2

Mary—Luke 1:46-55

Jesus—Matthew 11:25-26; Luke 10:21

Paul—2 Corinthians 1:3-4; Ephesians 1:3-14

Peter—1 Peter 1:3-5

Praise and Worship

>   Job—Job 1:20-22
>   David—2 Samuel 7:18-29; 1 Chronicles 17:16-27
>   Nebuchadnezzar—Daniel 4:37
>   Others—Psalms 8, 14, 67, 92, 95-98, 100, 113, 145, 148,
>   150; Revelation 4-5, 19:1-10

For Guidance and Wisdom

>   Eliezer—Genesis 24:12-14
>   Solomon—1 Kings 3:6-9
>   Psalm 25

Confession

>   Job—Job 42:1-6
>   Israel—Ezra 9; Nehemiah 9
>   David—Psalm 51
>   Publican—Luke 18:10-13

Doxologies and Benedictions

>   Genesis 31:49; Numbers 6:24-26; 1 Kings 8:57-58;
>   Psalm 19:14; Romans 15:5-6, 13, 33; 16:25-27; 1 Corin-
>   thians 1:3; 2 Corinthians 13:14; Ephesians 6:23-24;
>   Philippians 4:7-9; 2 Thessalonians 1:11-12; 3:16, 18;
>   1 Timothy 1:2; Hebrews 13:20-21; 1 Peter 5:10, 11, 14;
>   2 John 3; Jude 24-25; Revelation 1:4-6

Acknowledgment of Character of God

>   Psalms 8, 23, 29, 37, 91, 107, 139, 146

Personal Petitions

>   Gideon—Judges 6
>   Hannah—1 Samuel 1
>   Elijah—1 Kings 18
>   Hezekiah—2 Kings 20
>   David for Solomon—1 Chronicles 29

Public Dedications

>   Temple—1 Kings 8-9
>   Jesus—Luke 2:21-38
>   Walls of Jerusalem—Nehemiah 12:27-47

Patriarchal Blessings

    Isaac—Genesis 27

    Jacob—Genesis 48-49

Intercession

    Abraham for Lot—Genesis 18:22-33

    Moses for Israel—Exodus 32; Numbers 14

    Samuel for Israel—1 Samuel 7

    Nehemiah for Jerusalem—Nehemiah 1

    Jesus for Disciples—John 17

    Paul for Israel—Romans 10:1

    Paul for Churches—Ephesians 1:16-23; 3:14-19; Philippians 1:3-11; Colossians 1:3-14

Lament

    Jeremiah for Jerusalem—Lamentations 1-4

    David's Personal Laments—Psalms 10, 35, 38, 77

Questioning God

    Job—Job 10, 13-14

    Habakkuk—Habakkuk 1

    Jesus—Matthew 26:36-44; Mark 14:32-39; Luke 22:39-46

Longing for God

    Moses—Exodus 33

    Others—Psalms 16, 27, 42, 63, 84

Commitment to God

    Jacob—Genesis 28

    Israel—Nehemiah 9:5-38

    Isaiah—Isaiah 6

Prayer for Immediate Help

    Peter—Matthew 14:22-33

    Jairus—Matthew 9:18-26

    Others—Psalms 46, 66, 86, 88, 102, 140, 143

PRAYER STUDY WORKSHEET

SCRIPTURE REFERENCE: (Read it through at least once.)

BACKGROUND MATERIAL:
  Time and place:
  Customs:
  Sequence of events that lead to this prayer:
  Person offering the prayer:

REPEATED WORDS AND PHRASES:

NAMES GIVEN TO GOD:

THEME OF THE PRAYER:

ELEMENTS OF PRAYER INCLUDED:

LESSONS LEARNED FOR MY OWN PRAYER LIFE:

PARAPHRASE:

LESSON 9

Studying a Poem

Belinda loves poetry. Grace detests it. Andrea did not think she liked it until her daughter started to write it. Then she began to study it and found she could appreciate it. All three women are avid Bible students, and in spite of their opinions about poetry, not one of them dislikes the poetry she reads in her Bible. Even Grace finds it most fascinating. Like many Bible lovers, those three women were all amazed to learn that many of their favorite passages were poetic literature.

Did you know that one-third of the Old Testament is written in the form of Hebrew poetry? Most of it is in the five books we normally classify as poetic books—Job, Psalms, Proverbs, Song of Solomon, and Ecclesiastes. But much of it is also scattered throughout the Old Testament prophets.

In addition, large portions of the words of Christ and the apostles are highly poetic writing, even though they were not originally intended as poetic in form. Surely, in the face of such evidence, we must believe that God enjoys poetry. When He tells us that all Scripture is profitable for us, that must mean He intends for us to study His poetry as diligently as we do His prose.

At this point, those of you who are not poetry lovers may be asking why God used so much of it. Perhaps you consider poetry as a frivolous and impractical literary form. Since the Bible is a practical book, you wonder why it does not consist only of utilitarian, factual, teaching prose.

The answer is simple. First, God did indeed design His Book to meet human needs. As we have already seen, this includes the need for stories. One of our strong needs is the feeding of our emotional, aesthetic senses. Many needs in this area could never be met by prose—either sermons or stories. Being made in the image of God, we share His emotions and relate to Him in part through them. Any book of His dealings with us that would omit the use of emotion-based poetry would be an incomplete and faulty representation of God's Person and truth.

Further, there are times when dealing with a problem or a blessing when we come to a point where we are nearly speechless with our deep thoughts. We talked about that when we described worship on paper. At such times it may be that only poetic words will help us crystallize our thinking and arrive at practical, workable solutions. I once heard a Bible teacher comment on the poetry of Job: "Who of us has not felt much as Job did at some time in our lives? But how few of us have expressed our misery with such eloquence!"

Much of the poetry in the Bible falls into this category—misery or ecstasy expressed with eloquence. In the process it enables both the poet and the reader to work through their problems and find both comfort and solutions. What could be more practical?

If we are to understand and profit from the poetry of the Bible, we need to do three things: (1) define poetry, (2) examine the unique characteristics of biblical poetry, and (3) learn the steps to study it.

What is poetry? Because it is the most personal form of written expression, poetry means many things to many people. The number of definitions is endless. For our purposes, I have chosen one of my favorites, which not only defines but also demonstrates the meaning that I think will be most helpful for us.

A poem
is
a tiny shell
that whispers
all
the secrets
of
the sea.

John D. Engle[1]

Have you ever held a shell to your ear? As you listen, you hear a whisper of the sea. If you close your eyes and let your imagination carry you along, the sound gets bigger and bigger until you feel that you are actually standing on the beach, watching the waves, feeling the spray on your face, tasting the salt, even listening to the gulls scream above the now-deafening roar of angry breakers.

That is what a poem does. As you read it, your imagination takes the raw materials provided by the poem, combines them with your past experiences and emotional responses, and leads you to feel that you have shared intimately with the poet. As you discover what you have in common with the poet, you are encouraged and strengthened for dealing with the demands of life.

The shell itself is beautiful. So is the poem. Their power, however, lies not in beauty for beauty's sake alone, but in the message they allow your heart and mind to hear, see, feel, taste, and touch. Theirs is not a shouting message. Sermons shout. Poems whisper, in such a way that you feel you have discovered the truth for yourself.

What makes the poetry of the Bible unique? In many ways, biblical poetry is quite like nonbiblical poetry. In other ways, it differs in varying degrees. First, like many thought-provoking poems we read today, much biblical poetry needs to be re-read two or three times in order to get the full meaning. In fact, most of the Bible—poetry and prose—falls into that category.

---

1. First appeared in *Sunday Digest,* © 1975 by David C. Cook Publishing Co., Elgin, Ill. 60120. Used by permission.

We get an idea of the message from a first reading. The more we study, the more deep meanings and wide range of applications we discover. That kind of poetry is meant not for hasty perusal, but for diligent exploration.

Second, poetry comes in many forms. Biblical poetry is no exception. Most of the poems in the Bible are lyrical, written essentially to be sung, often to the accompaniment of instruments. Because Hebrew poetry is more rhythmic than melodic, it contains frequent repetition of phrases and refrains. In the Bible, we also find dramas, dirges, idyllic pictures, and exalted odes.

The Bible treats a variety of themes in poetry as well. The majority center on nature, praise, and worship. It is fascinating that biblical nature poems never praise nature. Rather they serve as a beautiful frame for a window through which we get an enhanced view of the God of nature.

Another common theme is the lament, in which a poet pours out the bitterness, depression, and grief of heart on a God whom he is certain can and will help him.

Confession occurs frequently as a poetic theme. Nothing matches poetry for its power to expose the remorse of a guilt-ridden soul. Finally, many poems have prophetic themes— God's promises of blessing for faithfulness and judgment for sin, as well as Messianic poems that predict the coming of Christ the Messiah.

At the end of this lesson, we have included a listing of the categories of biblical poetry, along with a few representative examples of each one.

A third thing that biblical and modern poetry share is their intent. C. S. Lewis summarizes nicely, "The psalms are poems, and poems intended to be sung; not doctrinal treatises, nor even sermons. . . . They must be read as poems if they are to be understood . . . . otherwise we shall miss what is in them and think we see what is not."[2]

While our Sunday school class was studying Psalms, a

2. C. S. Lewis, *Reflections on the Psalms* (New York: Harcourt, Brace, and World, 1958), pp. 2-3.

woman asked, "Psalm 37:25 says, 'I have been young, and now I am old; yet I have not seen the righteous forsaken or his descendants begging bread.' Is this a promise for us to claim in all our experiences?"

One class member reminded us that those words were the testimony of David's heart, and not a dogmatic pronouncement of divine doctrine. "It may well be that the Lord will use this verse to speak comfort to our hearts and promise us that He will take care of us in a given circumstance," our teacher explained. "But no, it is not a promise we can hold over God's head when things go badly for us."

If we are to understand the poetry of Scripture, we must learn the difference between a sermon and a poem. Remembering that the poem is the whispering shell and the sermon is the thundering wave helps us to put it into perspective.

Fourth, all poetry, biblical and nonbiblical, has an emotional emphasis and appeal. One writer says of Old Testament poetry, "The essence of this poetry is that it has great matters to convey forcibly to people of all kinds."[3] The content of biblical poems, unlike that of some nonbiblical poetry, is always highly significant. But we can always count on it to be handled on the emotional level.

Fifth, biblical poetry, like most nonbiblical poetry, is the voice of intensely personal experience. Rather than standing aloof from personal contact and looking at touchy issues, it opens up the heart of the poet and lays it all out for us to read and identify with. When David was plagued by unconfessed sin, he did not philosophize about the sure results of not dealing with sin. Rather, he said,

> When I kept silent about my sin, my body wasted away
> Through my groaning all day long.
> For day and night Thy hand was heavy upon me;
> My vitality was drained away as with the fever-heat
>   of summer.
>
> Psalm 32:3-4

---

3. David Alexander and Pat Alexander, *Eerdman's Handbook to the Bible* (Grand Rapids: Eerdmans, 1973), p. 317.

That is an admission of such an intimate nature that apart from poetry, no man would be likely to share it with anyone but God. Because poetry is such a personal art form, it reveals much about the poet. The more transparent he is willing to be on paper, the more we learn about him.

Sixth, biblical poetry illustrates the fact that the basic unit of the poem is imagery. In this, the poem differs from both the story and the sermon. A story moves from scene to scene. A sermon moves from point to point. The poem depends on a series of brief, concrete word pictures that help us understand abstract truth.

Psalm 91:1-2 illustrates that beautifully:

He who dwells in the shelter of the Most High

Will abide in the shadow of the Almighty.

I will say to the Lord, "My refuge and my fortress,

My God, in whom I trust."

If we read the story passages of 1 Samuel, we see the truth of those verses enacted in scenes as we watch David fleeing from Saul, yet always rescued as he trusted God and honored Him by doing things in His way. Those same verses could be summarized in one sermonic sentence, "If I trust Him, God will protect me." When the psalmist wrote about it, he wanted to enlarge upon the idea, make it more complete, exciting, and easier to identify with. So he gave us the imagery of a man hiding in the refuge of a great and powerful shadow in the heat of a summer desert. That enables us to bring our total persons into the poetic experience and gain security from our assurance of the protectiveness of God, in an intensely practical and personal way.

Finally, there is one area where we find the greatest difference between biblical and nonbiblical poetry. That is in the structure. Most modern Western poetry has been influenced by Greek and Roman writers and relies on rhyme and rhythm. Not all modern poetry has rhyme and rhythm as we think of them. But the ideal contained them both. And even no-rhyming, free-verse poetry has a type of thought rhythm not found in most scriptural poetry.

The basis for structural design in biblical poetry is known as parallelism. It is simply a balance of ideas and thoughts. Parallelism says the same thing in two or more ways. If you read about it in a Bible dictionary or encyclopedia, you may find a detailed analysis with many different kinds of parallelism. For our purposes, it is sufficient to recognize three basic types.

Synonymous parallelism means that the second line repeats the first line, only in different words, often using different imagery. For example,

> Has He said and will He not do it?
> Or has He spoken and will He not fulfill it?
>
> Numbers 23:19, RSV*

Or,

> Deliver me, O Lord, from the evil man;
> preserve me from the violent man.
>
> Psalm 140:1, KJV

For other examples, see Proverbs 8:22-29; Psalms 54, 104; Matthew 7:2; and Numbers 6:24-26.

Antithetical parallelism contrasts the second line with the first. They never contradict, but show two sides of a truth.

> The young lions do lack and suffer hunger;
> but they that seek the LORD shall not
> want any good thing.
>
> Psalm 34:10, KJV

> The LORD knoweth the way of the righteous,
> but the way of the ungodly shall perish.
>
> Psalm 1:6, KJV

For other examples, read through the book of Proverbs.

Climactic parallelism means each line adds something to the first, in such a way that a truth is gradually presented. For example,

---

Revised Standard Version.

For my thoughts are not your thoughts,
neither are my ways your ways, says the

LORD.
Isaiah 55:8, KJV

And he shall be like a tree planted
    by the rivers of water,
that bringeth forth his fruit in his
    season;
his leaf also shall not wither;
and whatsoever he doeth shall prosper.

Psalm 1:3, KJV

For other examples, see Matthew 7:7-8 and Ecclesiastes 3:1-8.

Parallelism is an effective technique for impressing truth on readers' minds. If I say a thing once, you may or may not get it. If I repeat it, using a little different imagery, you get a second chance and are more likely to remember what I have told you. The idea of repetition with a difference keeps us listening, and helps us to understand.

With that as a background, how, then, shall we study a Bible poem? First, read through the entire poem to get a broad overview. Then use the following worksheet. For our example, we will study Psalm 1. Instructions are enclosed in parentheses. Sample entry materials are italicized.

<u>BACKGROUND:</u> (For many of the psalms there is no background or context. Most of the other biblical poems have a context to study. If there is none, go on, but if there is, stop and study it.)

No background given. It is significant that this psalm appears first in the book—a song that emphasizes the ultimate value of godliness.

<u>EMOTIONS OR PROBLEMS OF THE POET:</u> (One key to emotions is the strong exclamations uttered by the poet. Problems come through in questions and laments.)

Psalmist delights at seeing the righteous blessed and prospered. Key exclamation: "How blessed is the man . . ."

REPEATED WORDS AND PHRASES: (Tools that help to find the theme.)

wicked or ungodly, righteous

THEME: (Central message in a single sentence. You may fill this blank in at the very end of your study, if it takes that much study to enable you to find the theme.)

The righteous are to be blessed and rewarded; the ungodly will be judged.

IMAGERY:

Verse 1—Walking, standing, sitting—Not literally intended, but figuratively, as a way of life.

Verse 4—Chaff being separated from wheat, as illustration of separating true from false followers of God.

(Other examples of imagery in this psalm—vv. 2, 3, 5)

PARALLELISM:

Synonymous—Verses 2, 5
Antithetical—Whole psalm is a contrast
Climactic—Verses 1, 3

HYPERBOLE: (This is a literary term for exaggeration for the purpose of making a point. We get into trouble when we try to take literally the extreme statements that do not square with other scriptural teachings.)

Verse 3: "Whatsoever he doeth shall prosper" does not mean the righteous will never know failure, problems, or reversals. Such an idea is contradicted by other Scriptures. Emphasis is on fruitfulness. In this bit of hyperbole, the psalmist is saying that when it comes down to the end, all a righteous man does leads to ultimate prosperity (cf. Romans 8:28).

LESSONS LEARNED: (These will be personal and may not cover every lesson in the poem—only those that meet your immediate needs.)

I must stay out of the way of the wicked man's influences— not even listen to his counsel. Instead, I must make God's Book my chosen companion and guide.

COMMITMENT: (Based on lessons learned, write a verbal commitment to God in the form of a prayer or a paraphrase.

Include intentions to obey, pleas for help to understand or obey, and plan of responsive action.)

Lord, guard me against the insidious invasion of wicked influences into my life. Keep me from listening to the advice of the ungodly and adjusting myself to their viewpoint.

(Record as little or as much as you feel is necessary to make this lesson practical. If you like, try rewriting the poem in poetic form. Experiment, be yourself, make this lesson express your heart at the deep levels of relationship with God.)

ASSIGNMENT:

1. Look through the following list of samples of different kinds of biblical poetry. Read some samples to get the feel for different types.

2. Using the Poetry Study Worksheet, study Psalm 23. For background material, refer to all you know about David's life. This psalm was not written in connection with any specific event that we know of. It was probably written late in his life. The more you know about his life, the better you will understand the poem. (His story is found in 1 and 2 Samuel.)

POETRY STUDY WORKSHEET

SCRIPTURE REFERENCE:

BACKGROUND:

Time and Place:
Author:
Reason for this poem:

EMOTIONS OR PROBLEMS OF THE POET:

REPEATED WORDS OR PHRASES:

THEME:

IMAGERY:

PARALLELISM:

HYPERBOLE:

LESSONS LEARNED:

COMMITMENT:

CATEGORIES AND SAMPLES OF BIBLICAL POETRY

Lyric poems: Short, personal poems, high in emotional content, usually, though not always, intended to be sung.
(Genesis 2:23; Ruth 1:16-17; Psalms 1, 23, 46)

Lament poems: Lyric poems expressing some sorrow or complaint. May be either long or short.
(Psalm 8, 10, 35, 77, 137; Lamentations; Matthew 23:37-39)

Praise poems: Praise response to works of God.
(Exodus 15:1-19; 1 Samuel 2:1-10; Psalms 18, 30, 66, 147-150)

Odes: "Lyric poems that treat a lofty subject in an exalted style."[4]
(Psalms 32, 90, 107, 139; 1 Corinthians 13)

Worship poems: Poems that exalt God as a response to His Person and character.
(Psalms 27, 42-43, 84, 134; Isaiah 40; Romans 8:31-39)

Nature poems: Poems that praise the God of nature for His might, creativity, and providence.
(Psalms 8, 19, 29, 104, 148)

Idyllic or pastoral poems: Quiet, ideal pictures of life at repose, depicting the goodness of the simple life. Usually use shepherds and rustic settings.

---

4. Leland Ryken, *The Literature of the Bible* (Grand Rapids: Zondervan, 1974), p. 157.

(Psalm 23; Song of Solomon; Isaiah 41:17-20; Ezekiel 34)

Benediction poems: Prayers for God's blessings to be showered on someone for some special reason.

(Numbers 6:24-26)

Confession poems: Lyric poems in which the poet offers a deep confession of sin and shallowness in his life. He usually pleads for restoration to fellowship.

(Job 42:1-6; Psalm 51)

Dramatic poems: Poems that tell a story.

(Judges 5; Job; Psalm 106)

Prophetic poems: Poems that share God's prophetic utterances with His wayward people, or that give a prophetic picture of the Messiah.

(Isaiah 5; Hosea 14)

Messianic poems: Poems that give a prophetic picture of the nature or mission of the coming Messiah.

(Psalms 22, 24, 40; Isaiah 53)

LESSON 10

Studying a Parable

If you were to write a list of the Bible stories you know best, no doubt you would include several parables. Probably you would at least list the Good Samaritan and the Prodigal Son. Those stories are so familiar that the terms *prodigal* and *good Samaritan* have become household words in the American language.

When we studied Bible stories, we discovered that God is the Great Storyteller. In order to communicate His heart to earth-bound men and women, He has told us stories that put human flesh on the bones of truth He wants us to learn. Not only does He tell real stories of real people functioning in historical situations, but in the parables, He shows Himself to be the Master of fiction technique as well. The parables were products of Jesus' human imagination collaborating with His divine nature in an attempt to share heavenly truth at a practical, earthly level.

When He sat on the hillside and looked at lilies, He said, "And why are you anxious about clothing? Observe how the lilies of the field grow; they do not toil nor do they spin, yet I say to you that even Solomon in all his glory did not clothe himself like one of these" (Matthew 6:28-29).

When His self-righteous, discourteous host, Simon, complained at a sinful woman's act of penitence and devotion, He told the story of two debtors (Luke 7:36-50). After Zaccheus's conversion He told the religious leaders the story of the pounds, or talents (Luke 19:1-27).

A parable is a simple, homey illustration drawn from the common circumstances of daily life, designed to add a spiritual dimension and sense of purpose to our otherwise mundane existence.

In Greek, the word *parable* means "putting things side by side" for the purpose of comparison. Jesus put the woman who lost her coin beside God the Father in order to show us how much He grieves over a lost soul. The parable is imagery extended into a plotted story.

A parable is a specific literary form. But the term is also used generally to refer to a variety of similar literary forms. First is the *simile* and its close cousin the *metaphor.* A simile is a mini-parable. The book of Proverbs is filled with them. "As cold waters to a thirsty soul, so is good news from a far country" (Proverbs 25:25, KJV). In that one brief sentence, the author compares two things to help us understand an abstract concept. Good news from a far land refreshes the spirit as well as cold water refreshes the thirsty body. This simile stimulates our imagination and senses so we appreciate the value of a letter we need to write to a friend far from home.

Second is the true *parable,* which takes a simile or a metaphor and turns it into a story. It tells an actual story of a traveler tramping through a hot desert, about to die from heat, thirst, and exhaustion. Lo, by some providential miracle, he finds an oasis with a well of cool water, and his ebbing life is restored to newness so he can resume the journey. The parable illustrates a single thought, and all the details of the story simply paint the picture vividly so that you can vicariously experience the story and understand its message.

A third literary form commonly thought of as a parable is the *allegory.* An allegory, such as *Pilgrim's Progress,* is a story in which each person, name, place, and detail has a special significance. In the parable, when you talk about the man walking through desert sands in 150 degree temperatures and wearing holey sandals, there is no special meaning to the temperature or the holes in the sandals. In the allegory, the holes in the sandals signify either poor preparation for the journey or an unexpectedly long journey (perhaps he was lost!). The desert would probably have a name such as Despair or Confusion. The man would most likely be named Wanderer or Rebel or some such identity-carrying tag.

Finally, there are *fables,* which are fanciful stories whose characters are animals and plants instead of people.

The Bible uses all four forms. In the Old Testament, we find mostly similies, with a few parables, allegories, and fables. Most biblical parables were told by Jesus and recorded in the first three gospels—Matthew, Mark, and Luke. Jesus told a few allegories, but usually when He did so, He ended them by interpreting each symbolic feature for His listeners. The story of the sower is an allegory. Here Jesus identified the sower as God, the seed as the Word, the field as the world. Then He explained the significance of the different types of soil.

Jesus also used a number of metaphors. We find them particularly in the book of John, where He did not actually tell parables. The word pictures He used throughout John were among the most graphic metaphors in all literature. "I am the Door" (John 10:9), "the Light" (John 9:5), "the Vine" (John 15:1), and "the Good Shepherd" (John 10:14). One of the chief characteristics of the book of John is its seven *I ams,* each revealing something special about Jesus as God's Son, who was prepared to meet human needs.

Why did Jesus use so many parables? If He had strong things to say and wanted to say them forcibly and with unmistakable clarity, why did He not stand up and preach from a pulpit, shouting at His listeners to repent and follow Him? John the Baptist preached that way. "If you have two coats," he thundered at his audience, "take one off and give it to the man who doesn't have any!" (Luke 3:11, my paraphrase). Why was Jesus, by contrast, so soft-spoken most of the time?

We need to remember that God called John the Baptist to be a fiery preacher. Jesus' calling was different. As a daily minister among men and women, He was first of all a walking demonstration of how God expects His human creatures to live. As God's verbal spokesman, He was most often a teacher. When He taught in parables, He was using one of the basic laws of teaching: take a student from where he is and gradually lead him where you want him to go. Jesus knew His listeners and started with the kinds of things they knew about and felt comfortable with. Being Hebrews, they spoke a language that had few abstract words and depended on concrete words to communicate such concepts. They were also a highly practical, earthy, functional people. They did not define ideas in lofty terms. They would describe love by painting pictures of love acting for another's benefit rather than in philosophical phrases and complex arguments.

Because Jesus was well aware of that, He did not command them, "Thou shalt have faith in God!" and let it go at that. Rather He told a parable:

"Now suppose one of you fathers is asked by his son for a fish; he will not give him a snake instead of a fish, will he? Or if he is asked for an egg, he will not give him a scorpion, will he? If you then, being evil, know how to give good gifts to your children, how much more shall your heavenly Father give the Holy Spirit to those who ask Him?" (Luke 11:11-13).

Jesus used parables to illustrate most of the major truths He taught during His ministry. As He spoke in parables, He was trying to teach two basic things—what God is like and how He expects us to live.

Remember, He had an audience of meticulously religious people. They were not atheists or materialists or idolators. They practiced an elaborate system of sacrifices and rituals directed to Jehovah, the one true God of Israel. As they paid fastidious attention to God's ceremonial laws, however, they failed to see what God was really like. They were too hung up on the regulations of the Mosaic law to grasp the spirit of that law. Jesus came into the world to fill the gaps in their understanding, to bridge the chasm between law and grace, to fulfill the Old Testament, or covenant, and usher in a new covenant between God and man.

With that goal in view, Jesus taught in parables that opened up the heart of God and laid it out for all to see. When taken together, the parables constitute what one writer calls "the autobiography of God."

Parables are more than God's autobiography, though. With their strong emphasis on ethics, they also show us that, in God's eyes, how we live is as important as what we believe, how many church services we attend, or how much money we put in the offering.

No study of Jesus' teachings about God and personal morals could be complete or understandable without some degree of mastery of these imaginative, practical jewels of literature we call parables. As teaching tools, they helped to prepare the hearts and minds of the Jewish nation for what was to happen at Calvary. Jesus' death was designed to usher in a new way of living and looking at things, based not simply on moral deeds, but on the wellspring of those deeds—the attitudes of the heart. As Jesus said in the Sermon on the Mount, the Law stated, "An eye for an eye, and a tooth for a tooth. But I say to you, do not resist him who is evil; but whoever slaps you on your right cheek, turn to him the other also" (Matthew 5:38-39).

The full implications of many of the parables were not clear to any of His hearers before His death and resurrection. When He told the story of the wicked vineyard keepers (Matthew 21:33-46), His enemies understood that it was directed against them. Not until after Calvary did they understand how the death of the vineyard owner's son was a picture of what was going to happen to Jesus at their hands, or how God planned to take the vineyard from the Jews and give it to others.

Jesus' parables did different things for different people. To all who were responsive to Him in their hearts, parables clarified His truth. But to those who had set their hearts against Him, they made the truth even harder to grasp. In Mark 4:11-

12 He told His disciples, "To you has been given the mystery of the kingdom of God; but those who are outside get everything in parables, in order that while seeing, they may see and not perceive; and while hearing, they may hear and not understand."

Jesus' parables were simple, extemporaneously composed stories that spoke of common experiences to the common man. They were a type of folk literature. Jesus' approach offended the religious leaders of the day. They wanted profound theses and theological dissertations that rambled on above the heads of the people. Folk literature was beneath their dignity.

The masses of common folk reacted with warmth to the messages, however. Weary of the aloof attitudes and meaningless philosophizing of their leaders, they were hungry for divine truth. Jesus' words told them that God's kingdom was open to anyone who was willing to humble himself and accept His terms.

Many people today still stumble over the simplicity of God's Word—particularly the parables. Without receptive and humble attitudes, we too can miss the life-changing messages they contain. Further, if we do not exercise caution, we can easily misinterpret them and miss the point Jesus intended through each story.

How can we avoid those errors and properly study and interpret the parables of Scripture?

First, read all the accounts of the parable. Some of Jesus' parables are found in two or three of the gospels. In the chart at the end of this lesson, you will find each parable listed with all its references. Reading all the records is important, because sometimes they contain slightly different elements and emphases.

Next, consider the context in which Jesus told the parable. That is a basic rule of biblical interpretation and is particularly vital in parable studies. You need to glean five things from the context:

1. The occasion. The parable of the Good Samaritan, for example, was an answer to a specific question. Find out what that question was.

2. Other teachings surrounding the parable. Sometimes the occasion is omitted, but parables are given in clusters or as part of a teaching section. Study them all and determine how your parable fits into the series or what sermon point it illustrates. For example, the parable of the soils (Mark 4:3-20) is the first in a cluster on seed planting. Each one adds something to the others.
3. Person to whom it was addressed. The parable of the wicked vineyard keepers (Matthew 21:33-46) was told to self-righteous Pharisees as a way to impress an uncomfortable truth on their proud hearts.
4. Special customs. The parable of the lost coin (Luke 15:8-10) has special significance, which a study of marriage customs will reveal.
5. Interpretation given by Jesus. The parable of the sower and soils (Mark 4:3-20) includes a full interpretation of each part of the story. Others, such as the parable of the lost sheep (Luke 15:3-7), end with a statement of intended meaning: "In the same way, there will be more joy in heaven over one sinner who repents than over ninety-nine righteous persons who need no repentance" (Luke 15:7).

Next, as you study the parables, follow three important rules of interpretation:

1. Accept the most natural and plausible interpretation. That keeps you from getting carried away with fantasy and turning simple parables into complex allegories. Bible students and theologians have often had trouble with this one. The classic example comes from the writings of the great church leader Augustine, who allegorized each detail of the Good Samaritan to the point of absurdity. In his exposition, "The unnamed man who went down from Jerusalem to Jericho is Adam. Jerusalem represents the Peace from which he fell and Jericho the human sinfulness toward which he was inclined. The thieves are the devil and his angels, who strip Adam of his immortality, beat him into sinfulness, and leave him half-dead. And so it goes through the whole parable, with Augustine finding some detail in the story of mankind which

he feels corresponds exactly with a minute detail of the parable."[1]

Following our rule would have saved Augustine a lot of trouble and enabled him to see the truth intended here. It will save you a lot of fruitless effort and confusion as well.

2. Do not look for truth that you cannot find anywhere else in Scripture. If you find an idea here that is not elsewhere, look again. You probably have confused what the parable is saying. Parables, like poems, do not stand alone in proclaiming doctrine. It is the work of sermons and epistles to preach doctrine. Poetry reacts to the doctrine, while parables illustrate it and occasionally prepare people to receive it.

3. Look for one main point in a parable. Do not search for two or three or ten or fifteen ideas. A parable may have several subpoints or explanatory angles to help make the central idea clear. But there is one point only. Lloyd Ogilvie, in his *Autobiography of God,* says that finding the key point to a parable is like finding the end strand in a ball of yarn. Once you find it, you can unravel the whole ball. Before that, you will make a dozen false starts that end in frustration and tangles.[2]

Finally, apply the truth of the parable to your specific circumstances, attitudes, and daily life. Based on the teaching you find, formulate in words your personal commitment to God. As you allow the parables to transform your life, this study is changed from an academic exercise into a valuable, personal encounter with the living God.

For our sample parable worksheet, we will look at the parable of the seed in Mark 4:26-29. Instructions are enclosed in parentheses. Sample entry materials are italicized.

CONTEXT:

Occasion: *Jesus was teaching multitudes by seashore. Crowd increased, and He got into a boat to teach from there.*

---

1. Kenneth E. Jones, *Let's Study the Bible* (Anderson, Ind.: Warner, 1962), p. 91.
2. Lloyd John Ogilvie, *Autobiography of God* (Glendale, Calif.: Regal, 1979), p. 7.

Other teachings surrounding the parable: *Parables of sower, candle under a bushel, mustard seed. Part of a cluster emphasizing living, growing aspect of kingdom of God.*

Persons to whom addressed: *Large crowd in Galilee.*

Special customs: *Crop planting done by broadcasting so that it fell on all kinds of terrain.*

Interpretation given by Christ: *None, though first parable in series was explained.*

MAIN POINT: (Read through the parable as many times as necessary to find this idea. May come as you do rest of study.) *God can be trusted to bring growth and life out of the seed we have planted.*

TEACHING ABOUT GOD: (What I see here depends on what I already know about God and what my immediate needs are. The same is true for the following categories of this worksheet. Hence, I may not see the same things my friend does when she studies the same parable. Also, I will see different things at different periods in my life.)

1. *God is faithful and trustworthy.*
2. *He is always on time in producing the harvest.*
3. *He is concerned about the seed and takes care of it.*
4. *He is powerful enough to nurture and protect the seed and bring it to the harvest.*

TEACHING ABOUT MAN:

1. *God chooses us to plant the seed.*
2. *We cannot hurry the growing process. Our part is to plant, water, cultivate, then go on with our business, leaving results with God.*
3. *People are extremely valuable to God.*
4. *God chooses us to reap the harvest.*

HOW MUST I LIVE?

1. *Because God is trustworthy, I can safely trust Him.*
2. *Because God is on time, I must stop worrying and wait patiently, while continuing to sow more seed.*
3. *Because God is concerned about the seed, I must not interfere with His nurture of it, nor play God in other people's lives.*

4. *Because God has chosen me to plant and harvest, I must be faithful in my performance.*

PRAYER OF COMMITMENT:

Dear Lord, take the troubled winds of my doubting, worried soul and breathe Your peace on them. I want above all to stop living in frustration where You have planned for me to rest in Your loving, concerned all-sufficiency to do all that You have promised to do with the seed that I have planted.

ASSIGNMENT:

1. Study the parable list following. Read as many samples as you want to or have time for.

2. Using the Parable Study Worksheet, study the parable of the unforgiving servant in Matthew 18:21-35.

3. On the Future Ideas Worksheet at the end of lesson 1 record other ideas for future parable studies as they occur to you.

PARABLE STUDY WORKSHEET

SCRIPTURE PASSAGE AND NAME OF PARABLE:

CONTEXT:

    Occasion:

    Other teachings surrounding the parable:

    Persons to whom addressed:

    Special customs:

    Interpretation given by Christ:

MAIN POINT:

TEACHING ABOUT GOD:

TEACHING ABOUT MAN:

HOW MUST I LIVE?

PRAYER OF COMMITMENT:

PARABLES OF THE BIBLE

I. SOME OLD TESTAMENT PARABLES
(Includes some fables)
Fable of the trees—Judges 9:8-15
Ewe lamb parable—2 Samuel 12:1-4
Fable of the thistle—2 Kings 14:9
Vineyard song—Isaiah 5:1-7
City under seige—Ecclesiastes 9:14-18
Wisdom in the streets—Proverbs 1:20-33
The strange woman—Proverbs 7:6-27

II. PARABLES OF JESUS

Name of parable	Matthew	Mark	Luke
Lamp under a bushel	5:14-15	4:21-22	8:16; 11:39
Houses on rock and sand	7:24-27		6:46-49
New cloth	9:16	2:21	5:36
New wine	9:17	2:22	5:37-38
Sower	13:3-23	4:3-20	8:5-18
Mustard seed	13:31-32	4:30-32	13:18-19
Tares and wheat	13:24-30		
Leaven (yeast)	13:33		13:20-21
Hidden treasure	13:44		
Pearl of great price	13:45-46		
Dragnet	13:47-48		
Lost sheep	18:12-14		15:1-7
Two debtors (unforgiving servant)	18:23-34		
Vineyard workers	20:1-16		
Two sons	21:28-31		
Wicked vineyard keepers	21:33-41	12:1-9	20:9-16
Marriage of king's son	22:1-14		14:7-24
Fig tree as sign of summer	24:32-33	13:28-29	21:29-32
Wise and foolish virgins	25:1-13		
Porter on watch		13:33-37	
Talents (pounds)	25:14-30		19:12-27
Sheep and goat judgment	25:31-36		
Silent growing seed		4:26-29	
Forgiving creditor			7:41-43
Good Samaritan			10:30-37
Friend in need			11:5-8

Rich fool	12:16-21
Watching servants	12:35-40
Faithful steward	12:41-48
Barren fig tree	13:6-9
Counting the cost	14:28-33
Lost coin	15:8-10
Prodigal son	15:11-32
Dishonest steward	16:1-8
Rich man and Lazarus	16:19-31
Master and his servant	17:7-10
Unrighteous judge	18:1-5
Pharisee and publican	18:10-14

LESSON 11

Studying a Biography

Biographies are exciting!

They open windows and doors into the personal lives and souls of people who have done significant deeds, thought significant thoughts, and experienced significant reactions to life. When we read biographies, we step into another time and another place, only to find ourselves on sometimes surprisingly familiar territory. All the differentiating barriers fade away as, with some historical character, we face problems, frustrations, and personal weaknesses very similar to our own. As we study the lives of the saints and sinners of the Bible we are encouraged as they affirm for us that we do not fight life's giants alone. They help us see our needs from an objective perspective and advise us in handling the things that perplex us.

The Bible is one of the richest sources of biographical materials in the world. It is filled with pictures of God interacting with men and women of all temperaments, ages, ranks, occupations, nationalities, and creeds. It shows us how God pursues His human creatures, how He provides for us, communicates with us, rewards our faith, judges our rebellion, and brings growth and purpose into our existence. When we study a biblical biography, however, we need to be aware that it is often different from the modern biographies we find on the library shelf. It is important that we understand five specific characteristics that make biblical biographies unique.

First, by today's standards, biblical biographies are incomplete. In a modern biography you expect to find all the details of a person's life—where he was born, where he grew up, what his parents were like, where his ancestors came from, and the like. The modern biographer shares with his readers the intricate secrets he uncovers about his subject's temperament, personality quirks, relationships, philosophy of life, and achievements.

When we read the Scriptures, we may be disappointed to discover that many of those details are missing. Some are simply not immediately evident and can be searched out with effort. As with all biblical truth, the deep things are reserved for the deep-sea divers and will not be revealed to the beachcomber.

Biblical biographies are sketchy because they are not written as biographies of men and women. Basically, like all other biblical literature, they are a part of God's biography. Every detail is chosen for the purpose of revealing some truth about God and His expectations of us. For that reason, many of the biographies of Scripture are nothing more than minibiographical sketches that show us one specific thing about the individual, usually in his relationship to God. Others tell two or three things.

In a few instances, God gives us quite a bit of material. Men such as Abraham, David, Moses, and Paul occupy large areas of biblical biographical narrative. Even in their stories, God selected only those things that teach us about Himself and how we, too, can live according to His plan.

It helps to remember that God never shares anything with us simply to satisfy our curiosity. He always has a deeper purpose. Even some of the basic kinds of personality traits we feel we ought to know in order to understand a person are missing. But we can be assured that He gives us all we need in order to enable us to know God better.

The best place in the Bible to look for brief biographical sketches is Hebrews 11. That fascinating series of minibiographies is held together by the common theme of how men and women acted when they believed and trusted God for the impossible circumstances of life. Almost all the subjects are people whose lengthier stories have been told elsewhere. Brought together, they form one of the literary masterpieces of the Bible. Hebrews 11 has been called God's Hall of Fame.

Biblical biographies are given to us as examples—some good, some bad. Paul tells us in 1 Corinthians 10 that the stories of the Old Testament are recorded to show us how we ought to live and understand God's demands upon us. Consequently, we find a lot of material about Jezebel, the scoundrel queen who did inestimable damage in the kingdom of Israel. Why would God choose to put her story in His book? Because she is such a fantastic example of the strength of a woman's influence and of how harmful that influence can be in our families and communities when we yield it to Satan rather than to God. Other stories of Scripture show us the benefits of a godly influence. We need to see how dangerous God's gifts can be when we fail to commit them to Him. How better to do that than to read about the Jezebels of history?

Second, in biblical biographies God is always the leading character. Modern biographies seek to exalt individuals for us to emulate or admire. The main purpose of biblical biographies is to bring attention and worship to God. "In studying a biblical character, we are seeing above all, God's impress upon him, a unique individual placed by Him in a particular environment among particular people."[1]

A friend of mine often reminds people that if we were to write Abraham's biography, we would shine the spotlight on the Abraham of God's choosing. Instead, God tells it as the story of the God of Abraham.

Knowing that unique characteristic of biblical biographies, we will always look for God in every biography found in His

1. Pamela White in John B. Job, *How to Study the Bible* (Downer's Grove, Ill.: Inter-Varsity, 1972), p. 46.

Book. If we do not, we will not only miss Him, we will miss the point of the biography as well.

Third, references to a biographical character are scattered. Trying to find all the pieces of a biblical biography presents a challenge. Basic historical facts are generally centered in one specific area. That is not true, however, of some people such as Peter and the other apostles, whose stories are spread throughout the four gospels and Acts.

Because their intent is not biographical, those stories appear in bits and pieces throughout the progressive plot of the Bible. Beyond the basic reference sections, however, you need to read all that other biblical characters said about your subject. By using a concordance you can look up every reference to the name you are studying. If he or she is known by another name as well, you can find the information in a Bible dictionary, concordance, or encyclopedia. Follow marginal references, as sometimes the person is mentioned elsewhere but not by name. For example, John the Baptist is prophesied specifically in several Old Testament passages, but not by name. As you read in John's story how he told his audiences that he was "the voice crying in the wilderness, Make straight the way of the Lord" (John 1:23, KJV), you will find a marginal reference to the Old Testament prophecy he is quoting. Or you may look up the prophecy in your concordance.

Fourth, the facts in biblical biographies do not always appear in chronological order. Occasionally that may be true of modern biographies as well. Often a biographer will begin telling his story at some crucial point, or with an incident that emphasizes the theme he has chosen to use. Apart from that, facts are usually centered on the life of a person, and we best grasp what happened when it is told in order as things happened. Chronological order helps us observe change and growth and understand the person's actions.

Because of its unique purpose, the order in which God presents the facts of a biblical biography is not keyed to time and character development as much as to the truth He wants to reveal through the story. One writer observes, "People were important, but the chronological details of their lives were not."[2]

We can learn many lessons from watching people grow in their relationships with God and other people. At times, when God intends for us to concentrate on those kinds of lessons, He presents the material chronologically. Hence, that type of approach is used in Scripture with great men such as Moses, Abraham, Jacob, David, and Paul. In other cases, such as John the Baptist, growth is not the important issue. Rather, John's life is presented as an example of how God chose a man for the unique mission of standing as a bridge between the Old Testament law-based system and the coming of Jesus Christ with His offer of grace. So, with John, the vignettes are sketchier than with Abraham, and the chronology is not as important.

Finally, biblical biographies are written from God's point of view. As a part of God's great autobiography, they show us how He sees every important area of life on planet earth— God, man, history, society, values, creation.

Those, then, are the distinctives of biblical biographies. With their special values in mind, it is easy to see why we need to study biblical biographies and mini-character sketches. How can we best do those studies and glean from them the truth God intends for us to apply to twentieth-century living?

First, choose a character to study. The reasons for our choices will be many. I once did a study of Barnabas because I suspected that he and I shared the same spiritual gift. I wanted to confirm my suspicion and learn what the gift consisted of and how it was worked out in his life. You may choose your subject for a similar reason.

Perhaps you want to know more about a topic such as faith. Since Abraham is used repeatedly in the New Testament as an example of faith, you may study Abraham in order to watch a positive example of the kind of faith God commended. Sometimes you choose a character you have always had a lot of questions about or you have especially admired. At other

2. Kenneth E. Jones, *Let's Study the Bible* (Anderson, Ind.: Warner, 1962), p. 55.

times you feel drawn to a character and are not satisfied until you know more about him or her. Perhaps you pick a person who faced a problem you are facing. Maybe you simply want a better understanding of some period in history.

Whatever your reasons, here are a few guidelines in making your choices:

1. In the beginning, choose someone whose story does not involve an overwhelming amount of material. Abraham presents a formidable challenge to beginners just because of the large volume of material available. Barnabas, on the other hand, comes in a manageable, non-threatening-sized package.

2. Do not despise the tiny studies. You cannot accurately judge the true depth of a person's life by counting the number of verses devoted to that life. Every biographical sketch is in the Bible for some useful purpose. Only as you tackle them will you find what that purpose is. Some of God's choicest gems appear ever so briefly in the biblical record.

3. Choose a variety of subjects. Do not study all women or all good characters or all leaders. Search out some of the obscure people, children, golden-age folks, and misfits of society.

Second, be prepared to spend some unhurried time with the character you choose. This is not a thirty-minute study that you pack into an odd chink of time on your lunch hour or as you are still prying your eyelids open before the household springs to life. While you may use some of those times for your study, do not expect to cram a complete study of Abraham or Moses or even Martha into one such mini-session. Plan on an indefinite number of such sessions. Then relax and work as long as it takes to become acquainted with your character and his or her God.

Third, find the Scripture references that cover your subject's story. With the help of a concordance and cross reference Bible, find all the references to him or her. Do not forget to include the sermons he may have preached, the prayers he may have prayed, the books he may have written. When you have completed the list, read them all through, in chronological order as much as possible. Also, if possible, do the whole reading at one sitting.

Fourth, gather background materials, using the enclosed Fact Worksheet. The more you know about your subject's environment, the better you can understand his actions. John the Baptist's actions and words would be totally out of place in modern America. When we study John and discover that he stood at the crossroads of cultures and at the time most ready for his revolutionary message, that changes our evaluation. In context, we get a clear picture of his coming and placement as a master stroke of divine planning.

Customs are particularly important to help you identify with your character so you can interpret what God did and said in his life in terms of what He wants to do and say in your life. When I studied Jochebed (Moses' mother), I learned that for a cradle for Moses, she no doubt used a strip of cloth or animal skin suspended from the ceiling by strong cord. Knowing that enabled me in my imagination to slip into her place. I thought about how silent such a cradle would be, and how imperative silence was as she hid her tiny infant son those three months. I felt the mounting pressure and the desperation that led her to trust God for the wildest of all plans. The ark in the bulrushes did not seem half so bizarre anymore. Reading about cradle customs did not give me all my insight. But it did open the door for me to pick up the insights with my mothering imagination.

Fifth, analyze your character, using the Character Worksheet. In the Fact Worksheet you meet your character. In the Character Worksheet you get acquainted with him and get some fresh glimpses of God.

Finally, apply lessons learned to your life situations, using the Application Worksheet. Look for examples of wrong actions, wrong attitudes, and errors of judgment as well as positive examples to emulate. However, remember that God does not want you to pattern your life after that of the character you study. Such patterning is a sure road to discouragement. When I was younger, I devoured all kinds of biographies. In the process, I became disillusioned, because they set some unrealistic expectations for me as I sought to follow them to the letter. God will not deal with you exactly as He dealt with any

Bible character. You are unique and He approaches you in the
one precise way that will best enable Him to produce His image in your life.

In the three sample worksheets that follow, instructions are
enclosed in parentheses. Sample entry materials are italicized.

BIOGRAPHICAL FACT WORKSHEET

NAME OF CHARACTER: *Barnabas*

REFERENCES:

*Acts 4:36-37; 9:26-30; 11:22-30; 12:25—15:39; Galatians
2:9-13; Colossians 4:10*

WHO?

Nationality: *Jewish, from tribe of Levi (Acts 4:36)*

Family: *Cousin of John Mark (Colossians 4:10)*

Occupation: *Church leader, missionary, teacher*

WHEN?

Political Situation: *Rome ruled the world.*

Religious Situation: *Church was being persecuted by both
Rome and the Jewish people.*

Everyday life and customs: (List those that affect your
story.)

*Many Jews had been dispersed throughout the Roman Em-
pire. That is how Barnabas and his family came to be living
in Cyprus.*

Who were his contemporaries? *Twelve apostles and Paul*

WHERE? (List all places where he lived, along with any significant features about those places.)

*Cyprus (lived as a dispersed Jew); Jerusalem (member of Je-
rusalem church); Antioch (missionary work with Paul);
traveled with Paul on his missionary journey; returned to
Cyprus as a missionary.*

WHAT?

Birth: (Conditions, place, anything unusual.) *Cyprus*

Childhood and training: (Often these are not given.)

Accomplishments:

1. *Sold property and gave money to church (Acts 4:37).*

2. *Introduced Paul to the church (Acts 9:27).*
3. *Worked with Paul in founding first Gentile church, in Antioch (Acts 11:22-26).*
4. *Gave John Mark a second try (Acts 15:36-39).*
5. *Went on missionary journey with Paul (Acts 13-14).*
6. *Took leadership in Jerusalem church matters (Acts 15:1-12).*

BIOGRAPHICAL CHARACTER WORKSHEET

WHO?

Meaning of his name: (Look this up in your concordance or dictionary. Sometimes names had a significance; sometimes not. If your subject's name fits the theme of his life then it has significance, otherwise ignore it and go on.)

Barnabas means "Son of Consolation." His real name was Joseph, and Barnabas was the name assigned to him by church members, hence it probably indicated something about how others saw him—an encourager.

How did he relate to his family? (May be important index to his character.)

Barnabas did a great deal to encourage and develop the gifts and character of his cousin, John Mark (Acts 15:36-39).

How did he relate to God? (Search his whole life for evidence of this. It won't be spelled out.)

Barnabas was sensitive to leading of the Holy Spirit and obedient. He trusted Paul when no one else was ready to do so because God told him to (Acts 9:27).

How did he relate to others?

Barnabas was an encourager of the brethren. Stood in the background and played a supportive role in the church. Spoke up occasionally.

WHEN?

Did he make a significant contribution to his times? (What will history remember this person for?)

Barnabas did not make his mark in history, but as a supporter of Paul, he was influential.

WHERE?

Was his character influenced by geography in any way?

First missionary journey was rough for geographical reasons. That made John Mark turn back. Barnabas became involved in giving him another chance.

Did he influence the communities where he lived?

Barnabas did, both in Antioch, Cyprus, and all the places he and Paul visited on their missionary journey.

WHAT?

His weaknesses: (Note reasons for these weaknesses.)

Barnabas was once led astray by Peter, probably because of his sensitive nature (Galatians 2:11-13).

His strengths:

Barnabas believed in people, took risks for them, shared with them, encouraged them, and prayed for them.

How did he face conflicts?

Barnabas did what he believed God wanted him to do, even when others disagreed with him.

Evidences of growth:

Was given increasing responsibility.

BIOGRAPHICAL APPLICATION WORKSHEET

WHO?

What can I learn from him about relating to God?

Be sensitive to the Holy Spirit more than to men.

What can I learn from him about relating to people?

Look at God's potential in a man and work with God to help him develop that potential.

WHEN?

How can I make a significant contribution to my times?

Only be faithful to God's calling and let Him worry about the scope of my contribution.

WHERE?

How can I best use my geographical location?

Serve God wherever He places me.

How can I influence my neighbors for God?

Be all that God asks and empowers me to be, and His influence will spread.

WHAT?

Can I identify with his weaknesses?

Yes, I need to be cautious not to let my sensitivity lead me off track.

Can I identify with his strengths?

I need more of his willingness to work quietly in the background.

What can I learn about handling conflicts?

He seemed to keep his perspective while under pressure. I need to learn this.

What does his life teach me about growth?

As I am faithful in using my gifts for God, He will increase my responsibilities.

PRAYER OF COMMITMENT:

Dear Lord, I desire never to forget that the gift of encouragement You have bestowed on me is not mine, but Yours. Teach me each day to live in such a way that this fine gift may be always a sharp and ready instrument for You to use in the lives of all You send to me needing Your comfort and direction.

ASSIGNMENT:

1. Using the three following worksheets, do a biographical study of Ruth.

2. Add to your Future Ideas Worksheet names of other persons you would like to study in the future.

BIOGRAPHICAL FACT WORKSHEET

NAME OF CHARACTER:

REFERENCES:

WHO?

Nationality:

Family:

Occupation:

WHEN?

Political Situation:
Religious Situation:
Everyday life and customs:
Contemporaries:

WHERE?

WHAT?

Birth:
Childhood and training:
Accomplishments:

BIOGRAPHICAL CHARACTER WORKSHEET

WHO?

Meaning of his name:
How did he relate to his family?
How did he relate to God?
How did he relate to others?

WHEN?

Did he make a significant contribution to his times?

WHERE?

Was his character influenced by geography in any way?
Did he influence the communities where he lived?

WHAT?

Weaknesses:
Strengths:
How he faced conflicts:
Evidences of growth:

BIOGRAPHICAL APPLICATION WORKSHEET

WHO?

What can I learn from him about relating to God?

What can I learn from him about relating to people?

WHEN?

How can I make a significant contribution to my times?

WHERE?

How can I best use my geographical location?

How can I influence my neighbors for God?

WHAT?

Can I identify with his weaknesses?

Can I identify with his strengths?

What can I learn about handling conflicts?

What does his life teach me about growth?

PRAYER OF COMMITMENT:

SUGGESTED BIOGRAPHICAL WORKSHEET

Adam	Hannah
Noah	Eli
Rebekah	Saul
Joseph	Josiah
Esau	Hezekiah
Jochebed	Jezebel
Miriam	Ezra
Aaron	Nehemiah
Joshua	Nebuchadnezzar
Caleb	John the Baptist
Rahab	John Mark
Samson	Samaritan woman
Gideon	Mary Magdalene
Deborah	Syrophoenician woman
Ruth	Jairus
Naomi	Andrew
Boaz	Thomas

Nicodemus   Matthew
Mary of Bethany   Philemon
Martha of Bethany   Priscilla
Lazarus   Agrippa
Zacchaeus

LESSON 12

Studying a Problem

"Never tell anybody that Jesus solves all our problems. Has He solved all of yours?"

The words stabbed at me from the page of a Christian magazine. I was shocked! Of course, Jesus could solve all my problems. I had been taught since I was a child that the Bible held all the answers I would ever need.

Those shocking words made me stop and think. I have returned to think of them many times since. At some stages in my life, when I was facing perplexing problems that seemed to defy solution, I have tended to agree with them. At other times I have insisted that Jesus does have all the answers. The germ of every one lies in the Bible. If I do not find them, the problem is in me, not in the Bible. If I am willing to do things God's way and diligent enough to search them out, surely I can find any answer I am capable of seeking.

Experience has taught me that this is largely true. However, I have also found that God knows it is good for us to keep some problems on the stewing burner. If He dispensed solutions to us like pills in a free clinic lineup, we would only cue up for medicines and stop communicating with Him as a Father. We will always face problems. He will always have answers. He shares His solutions with us, however, only as we are mature enough to obey His leading and handle the problems in His way. Sometimes He even has to show us that there are no simple, conclusive answers to some problems.

Some questions we will not even need to ask, once we get to know our Bibles and the character of God sufficiently well. With other questions, we will need to spend a lifetime wrestling our way through the Scriptures in order to find answers. At other times, we feel sure we know an answer. But as we study the Bible, we find that our solutions are far from adequate, too simplistic, or even far off course. The more we learn about God Himself, the closer we will come to finding solutions to life's problems.

Does the Bible have solutions to problems? Paul told Timothy that it does, "All Scripture is . . . profitable for teaching, for reproof, for correction, for training in righeousness; that the man of God may be adequate, equipped for every good work" (2 Timothy 3:16).

We all recognize that the Bible is our primary source of deep theological truth. We can go to its pages for a wealth of education on any topic of spiritual significance we can imagine. (Incidentally, the method we suggest in this lesson is good for pursuing any biblical topic, whether a problem or a doctrinal issue.) But we must be assured that the Bible is more than a doctrinal textbook. It is also an intensely practical guidebook that we can apply to every conceivable phase of daily living. That means it does indeed have answers to our problems and moral dilemmas.

How, then, does the Bible present those answers to us? In a variety of ways. First, there are direct answers. God's Word is full of commands to do or not do certain specific things. The Ten Commandments give us a foundation for that type of answer, but they are just the beginning, the summary of God's moral law. Hence, we need never ask whether it is right to take something that does not belong to us, because we have the direct command "Thou shalt not steal." Many other issues fall in this category as well.

Second, we find some general answers given in the form of

principles of godly conduct and attitudes. "Be anxious for nothing, but in everything by prayer and supplication with thanksgiving let your requests be made known to God" (Philippians 4:6). That is a clear principle that applies to a wide spectrum of different kinds of problems, all having the common denominator of worry. Put it together with "Casting all your care upon him, for he careth for you" (1 Peter 5:7, KJV), and you come up with an answer that should carry you through a multitude of trying problem situations in life. At least you should never need to ask, Is it right for me to worry over this thing?

Further, this principle is basic in understanding how to deal with all problems. It tells us that while there are problems we must wrestle with and work out solutions for, there are others that are His to solve. When we try to tackle those things that are His domain (e.g., changing other people's attitudes, engineering circumstances), we show that we are guilty of anxiety. To avoid that, we can learn to count on Him to handle His share of the load and give us specific guidance and strength to shoulder ours.

Finally, as a part of our answers, He promises us many supernatural enabling resources. These promises help us to find the solutions we seek. "If any of you lack wisdom, let him ask of God, that giveth to all men liberally, and upbraideth not; and it shall be given him" (James 1:5, KJV). "Peace I leave with you, my peace I give unto you" (John 14:27, KJV). "Come unto me, all ye that labor and are heavy laden, and I will give you rest" (Matthew 11:28, KJV). Those promises give us the courage to reach out and appropriate wisdom, peace, and rest—inner resources that God offers us from His vast spiritual reservoirs.

What kinds of problems does the Bible answer for us? We face two kinds of problems, and the Scriptures speak to both. First, there are the *moral problems.* Shall I steal or not steal? Some of these are clearly outlined in the Bible, and some are not so simple. Murder is clearly forbidden, but when it comes to abortion, we have to dig a bit deeper than the "Thou shalt not kill" of the Ten Commandments to be certain we know what God is saying, not just what we have always thought He was saying. Here, more than one moral issue is at stake. This happens often and requires maturity and sensitivity to the Holy Spirit to weed out truth from error.

Sometimes moral issues appear to contradict each other. Then we have to learn to balance such things as God's love and His justice. Parents must learn this in deciding how to function morally as godly guardians of the children God has entrusted to us as a stewardship. If we show our children only justice and no mercy, we will not be godlike. Yet, we know a child's sins must be punished. So we learn by watching God in action through the Bible, how to balance our moral obligations to exercise both justice and mercy.

Many of the problems we face are non-moral issues. These may be matters of guidance: Which job shall I take? Where shall we spend our vacation? Which dress shall I buy? In those kinds of matters, we want to seek to do the specific thing that will most please God. At times He will use His Word to give us guidance about arranging our priorities or how we ought to spend our money, which will in the long run affect our choice of job, vacation, dress, furniture, car, or whatever. At other times, it is a simple matter of our maturity level that enables us to be adequately sensitive to His daily nudgings of our spirits in the direction He wants us to move.

Another non-moral kind of problem we all wrestle with as we study the Bible is simply learning to understand difficult verses or biblical concepts. These are not matters of right and wrong, but again they arise from our experience with study and our maturity level. It is important to know that often Scripture is its own best explainer. If we leave certain puzzling problems on the back burner when we cannot find the answers, we will often discover them in some other study, when we are not looking for them.

Biblical solutions to human problems are based on two important considerations: the character of God and our moral obligation to God and one another.

If we have only vague, fuzzy pictures of what God is like, then decisions, particularly of a moral nature, are much more difficult to make. People who never bother to read their Bibles, except when they are in trouble and seeking quick answers to panicky situations, rarely find substantial answers. God does not give answers to those who want only answers. He gives answers to those who know Him and want to please Him.

When you were a child and you considered asking your father's advice, how often did you decide, "I know my father well enough to know just what he will tell me"? In like manner, if you know God as the provident, loving, concerned Father that the Bible portrays, you will immediately know that He does not want you to panic when your husband loses his job—or you lose yours. You know His character well enough to know that He will take care of you. You may have difficulty persuading your emotions to live with your head knowledge. But you have no need to wrestle through the Bible to help you decide whether you should sit and worry over your plight.

As you go through your Bible reading and studying, jot down in the back of your Bible a running list of the characteristics of God. Then, when you face a problem, look at your list. It will remind you that God is love. In a time of severe trial, that reminder enables you to trust a God who has committed Himself to your well being and will never allow anything to happen to you that is not the very best that could happen to you now. Perhaps you have disobeyed Him along the way and you are now suffering the consequences of that disobedience. Even then, His love is the characteristic that makes the suffering necessary. It is best for you to be made uncomfortable in order to learn obedience for the next situation. Your list will go on to include God's holiness, justice, redemption, sovereignty, mercy, position as Creator, and others.

Beyond knowing God's moral character, we need to be aware of our moral obligations to God and one another. The Bible tells us clearly that we are moral beings, capable of moral choices that will please God. We are stewards of God's world, dependent on each other, and responsible to seek one another's good ahead of our own. Most of all, we are capable of bringing glory and pleasure to God. Many of our problems will be solved simply by examining our motives in the light of our moral obligations.

When you have a problem and want to find a biblical solution, how do you go about it? First, identify the problem. You say, "But I already know what the problem is." Do you? Verbalize it. Put it on paper. In the process, you may find that it is not what you thought it was at all. Be specific. Cut all the vague, self-defensive verbiage and face the thing squarely.

Second, determine what caused your problem. Perhaps you believe someone else caused it. "She said a very unkind thing about me." Then, that was her problem. Your problem is not the other person's unkind words, but your disturbed reaction to her words. Why did it upset you? Was it your genuine concern for the other person, or simply your pride, jealousy, fear, insecurity, a grudge you hold, or your unwillingness to admit a failure? If you have brought the problem on yourself, sometimes this will give you the clue for solving it.

Third, ask yourself two questions: (1) Is there anything that I already know about the character of God that will give me my answer? (2) Is there anything I know about my moral obligations to God and others that will give me my answer? That may end your search.

Fourth, look up all that the Bible has to say about your problem. That may sound formidable, but it is really much simpler than you think.

Let's suppose you have decided that for you the problem over a friend's nasty words is really envy of her popularity. First, you take your concordance and look up the word *envy* in all its forms (envious, envied, envying, etc.). Make a list of all the references that use those words. If you find a note to "See also _____," look up the other words as well. Look also for words that are synonyms for your problem word. If fatigue is your problem, look under *weary, tired, faint*. Look also for those words that are the opposite of your problem or represent a solution you want to experience. If your problem is worry, look at *peace.* If envy, try *love.*

If you have a topical Bible, look up *envy* there as well. Once your list is complete, go through your Bible and find each reference. Jot down on a sheet of paper what each verse says about the subject.[1]

Finally, look at the end of the topical Bible listings and in the concordance for illustrations or examples of people dealing with envy in Scripture. Read each story carefully and decide what the example teaches you.

Fifth, go to the Problem-Solving Worksheet and fill in the blanks. As we search for divine solutions to human problems, we always need to exercise caution. Be sure to abide by all the rules for biblical interpretation that we have emphasized all through this course. Three areas pose special dangers for problem-solving studies:

1. Always consider each reference in context.

2. Never take any one verse as the final, conclusive answer to your problem without comparing it with other verses in other parts of the Bible. If a verse appears to contradict other Scriptures you have read, look at it again. You have probably misunderstood its meaning or its purpose.

3. Always check the New Testament teaching as the final authority on some controversial issue. God gave us the Old Testament as an example of His dealings with men and a foundation on which Christ built His church. Jesus came to fulfill the old law-based system with its rituals and combination of religion and state. He introduced in their place some radical new spiritual principles for godly conduct and structuring the church.

Many people today, not understanding this, claim God's promises of material prosperity to Old Testament saints for themselves. They miss two important things: (1) The Old Testament was based on God's covenant with a specific nation of

---

1. One little booklet that may be helpful to you is *The Personal Promise Pocketbook,* by Harold Shaw Publishers. It is purse- or-pocket size and gives you a good selection of verses for a long list of common problems.

people (the Jews) and centered on a land, a ceremonial law, and a God-controlled government. (2) Jesus' teachings continually emphasized the need to prepare ourselves for persecution in a world that would be hostile to Him and His Body, the church. He also talked about the need to set our hearts on spiritual priorities, not material values. He did assure us that He would provide for our needs, but prosperity was not in His vocabulary.

Your final step, after gathering and organizing all the applicable truths of Scripture, is to look back at your own specific problem and prayerfully consider the alternative actions you could take in solving it. Perhaps the right answer is clear. Sometimes, however, you will find two or more possible alternatives, at least in the initial stages of trying to interpret what is best. When you have considered the alternatives and decided on the solution that is best for you, write your prayer of commitment and request for enablement to live up to that commitment.

If you go through this whole process (remember, it may take several sessions of concentrated study) and are still uncertain what you should do or think, set it aside and continue to pray that the Lord will show you His answer in His time and way. At least now you are saturated with what His Word has to offer. At the proper time, when the circumstances of your life and commitment line up just right, He will enable you to put it all together in the way that pleases Him the most.

The three most important keys to remember in any problem-solving study are these: diligence in study, submissiveness to His will, and patience.

ASSIGNMENT:

1. Using enclosed Problem-Solving Worksheet, study the problem of worry.

2. Record on your list at the end of lesson 1 any other ideas that come to you for further problem-solving studies.

SAMPLE SHEET NOTING SCRIPTURE IDEAS ON *ENVY*

Job 5:2—Envy is self-destructive. Also Proverbs 14:30.

Psalm 37:1, 7—Don't envy prosperous wicked man. His time is coming. Also Proverbs 23:17; 24:1.

Proverbs 27:4—Envy is powerful.

Song of Solomon 8:6—Envy makes us do cruel things.

1 Corinthians 3:3—Envy is man's way of doing things, not God's.

1 Corinthians 13:4—Envy cannot coexist with love.

Galatians 5:19-21—Envy is wickedness.

James 3:14-16—Envy leads to confusion and all evil.

James 5:9—Don't hold grudges.

PROBLEM-SOLVING WORKSHEET

Identify Problem:

Envy

Cause of Problem:

Friend's popularity with my circle of friends. She seems to have more charisma with them than I. So when she speaks unkindly of me to them, I am envious.

Bible Says About My Problem:

Commands:

Don't envy prosperous wicked person—Psalm 37:1, 7
Don't hold grudges—James 5:9

Promises:

His time is coming—Psalm 37:2

Biblical principles:

Envy is self-destructive—Job 5:2
Envy makes us do cruel things—Song of Solomon 8:6
(I would also list the others found in 1 Corinthians, Galatians, and James—see jotting sheet.)

Biblical examples:

Jacob (Genesis 30)—led to deceit and theft and many

years of exile, also to broken family relationship.
Cain (Genesis 4) — led to first murder and Cain's exile.
(There are many others I would include here.)

Alternative Actions I Can Take:

1. *Retaliate with harsh words either to her face, behind her back, or both.*
2. *Confess my own envy, then go out of my way to be kind to her. (See examples of Joseph, David, Jesus.)*

God's Solution:

Alternative 2 above.

Prayer of Commitment:

Dear Lord, Cleanse my heart of the envy I feel toward my friend. Replace it with Your love. Enable me to show kindness to her in some practical way today. Set a guard before my lips that I may speak only well of her because I love her deeply and rejoice that You have allowed her to join my circle of friends.

PROBLEM-SOLVING WORKSHEET

IDENTIFY PROBLEM:

CAUSE OF PROBLEM:

BIBLE SAYS ABOUT PROBLEM:

Commands:

Promises:

Biblical principles:

Biblical examples:

ALTERNATIVE ACTIONS I CAN TAKE:

GOD'S SOLUTION:

PRAYER OF COMMITMENT:

FURTHER PROBLEM-SOLVING STUDY IDEAS

Disappointment with circumstances
Disappointment with loved ones
Fear
Discouragement
Worry about money
Bereavement
Loneliness
Rejection
Laziness
Sickness
Fear of death
Holding grudges
Fatigue
Tension
Worry
God's will
Failure
Facing a crisis
Assuming more responsibility
Family roles
Career choices
Temptation
Hunger

LESSON 13

Planning Bible Studies
for a Busy Schedule

Congratulations!

You have just achieved a monumental goal. During the past weeks, you have worked your way through twelve new Bible study adventures and increased your Bible I.Q. by a good many points!

As you proceeded, you always knew that when you finished one study, the format and assignment for another awaited you in the next chapter. Now at the end of your structured journey, you are asking: What next?

Along the way, you found many ideas you wanted to stop and pursue. Instead you jotted them down on a list, reserving them for another time. That *other time* has arrived. You review your list. Each idea stirs renewed excitement. About halfway down the page you begin to feel overwhelmed and confused.

Where shall you begin? Which one should you do first? How shall you decide? You wonder whether I can give you a one-year plan, a five-year plan, a ten-year plan, to guide you in your future Bible studies.

No, I cannot offer you a simple time-tagged plan of any sort. Nobody can design a plan for you. Bible study is intensely personal and individualistic. Only you can make a plan that will fit your needs and your study skills.

What I can offer you, however, are some guidelines to help you make those choices and experience the genuine wonder and exhilaration of a lifetime of personal, systematic Bible study discoveries.

First, begin at some point of need in your life. Are you facing a problem and need to search out the answer? Do you want to slip into a prayer closet with Moses or Elijah or Hannah and learn how to pray? Do you need an exposure to worship as expressed in the poetic passages? Is there a place in your reading where you want to stop and paraphrase it so you can be sure to get all the juice out of it? Are you anxious to get acquainted with Ruth or Joshua or Barnabas and come to understand his or her God more clearly?

The reasons for your specific choice will vary. Regardless of your motives, make sure your choices reflect a genuine need, not just an idle curiosity or a desire to become an authority on some subject or fill your arsenal with weapons to set somebody else straight on something.

Second, have a reading plan. In chapter 1, we talked about the difference between Bible reading and Bible study. Then through the remaining chapters, we tried to guide you into effective ways to study. We all need to save room in our schedules, however, for systematic Bible reading. It should not take the place of our studies. Rather, it enhances our studies by giving us a broader background of general Bible knowledge.

Many Bible study method books offer simple Bible reading plans. Each plan is different and has some strong merits. In Appendix 3, I have provided several plans for you. Which you choose will depend on your personality, your interests, your immediate needs. The important thing is that you pick a plan and stick to it. Do not read your Bible by the hop-skip-jump method. Be systematic in your approach.

In addition, let me suggest the following six short rules for Bible reading:

1. Read daily. Give it a regular time and place assignment.

2. Read with pencil in hand. Mark your Bible. Jot down surface observations, ideas, questions. Do not labor long at these jottings, however. That would be study.

3. Major on New Testament readings but do not neglect the Old Testament.

4. Reread the gospels most frequently. Read the Psalms often, too. Reading the gospels is vital because they show us a clear, close-up view of Jesus Christ. Read a psalm to open your day—or close it.

5. Whenever possible, read aloud. Hearing enables you to grasp what you read much more thoroughly.

6. Read with your family.

Finally, I want to give you a list of seven practical guidelines for planning your lifetime of Bible study:

1. Be realistic. Do not start with long, major kinds of studies—book studies, exhaustive topical studies, lengthy biographies. Start simply. If you bite off too big a project or start with Genesis and plan to move progressively through your Bible, you will likely become discouraged. Try something that is simple enough to match your skill level and will not threaten you each time you open your Bible.

Do not expect too much of yourself, particularly in the beginning. Do not let it bother you when you cannot accomplish all you had hoped for in a given study. Remember, there are no time limits, no final exams, and no report cards.

Do challenge yourself, however. Make your choices simple enough so they will not discourage you but difficult enough so that they will stretch you. In this way you will grow both as a person and as a Bible student.

2. Do not plan too far ahead. I cannot give you a ten-year plan. Neither should you try to make one for yourself. Our study needs change rapidly with the changing challenges of our lives. You may pick a study for now, with a project list of two or three others to follow in sequence. But it should never be considered a hard-and-fast commitment.

3. Be consistent and systematic. Study something every day. You may actually have two or three studies going at the same

time, but do them consistently. For example, perhaps you are studying a biography of Jonah on Monday through Friday. On Saturday you take a break and study a psalm or a parable. On Sunday you paraphrase a verse or cluster of verses.

Whatever system you choose, remember to put your Bible study at the top of your priority list.

4. Be flexible. No matter how beautiful your schedule, never make it so rigid that God does not have a chance to interrupt and surprise you with some special, well-timed study treat. At times, special needs arise that force you to depart from your pattern and do something different just for the need of the moment. You will find certain passages that you want to return to and re-study often as you wrestle with certain types of recurring challenges. Make room for those studies when the situation dictates. I find myself going back repeatedly to such passages as Psalms 27, 37; Isaiah 40:27-31; Matthew 11:28-30; Colossians 3:12-17; and several others.

When a study gets too difficult or you tire of what you are doing, it may be a signal that you are in over your head and need to move on to something else. Do not, however, just automatically change subjects every time you encounter a difficulty. Learn to use balanced wisdom.

5. Do not compare your progress with anyone else's, either in a group or among friends. It is not how much you learn compared to anyone else that counts. What is important is that you apply what you learn and grow to know God better.

6. Plan for variety. Study in both Old and New Testaments. Do different kinds of studies. Never let yourself slip into a rut with Bible study. Lack of variety kills spontaneity and restricts learning to a narrow range of experience. To do that to a book as big and exciting as the Bible is a *sin!*

7. Enjoy yourself! Bible study is not like most other things that are good for you. It is fun, stimulating—the most exciting thing you will ever do. So keep it on the adventurous side.

ASSIGNMENT:

1. Use the following Planning Worksheet to help you decide where you want to go next in your personal Bible study.
2. Pick a new Bible study topic and do it!

PLANNING WORKSHEET

Time slot for my study:

Place for my study:

Study methods I feel comfortable with:

Study methods I want to learn more about:

Study methods I cannot seem to handle at this point:

New study methods I want to experiment with:

Needs I feel in my life:

Specific studies that may help me to meet those needs:

Topics I have always wanted to learn more about:

Specific study I plan to do next:

APPENDIX 1

HELPS FOR TEACHERS OF THESE LESSONS

If you are a teacher responsible for leading a group in the use of these lessons, here are some suggestions:

1. Be prepared. Read the entire course through before you begin so you have an idea where it is going and what you will be covering. Work out the assignments yourself, preferably before you teach them. In that way, you will be better able to answer students' questions and help them understand what they are expected to do.

2. Be flexible enough to meet the needs of your class. If you do one lesson a week, you will finish in three months, which is one Sunday school quarter. However, be sensitive to the needs of your group. Perhaps they need more than one week to work out some of the lessons. If so, unless you are committed to a time frame, slow down and take the time needed. I suggest that you do not slow it too much, however, lest it become draggy. Probably you should not consider taking more than five or six months of weekly lessons. If your group meets once a month, consider one lesson a month for the year, since lesson 13 is not a full lesson in the sense that the others are.

3. Decide how you want to use the materials in your class. Here are three possible formats:

a. Use the textbook in class. Let students take turns reading different sections. Discuss them as you go along. Talk about sample assignments. Do assignments at home. Share findings at each session.

b. Have members read the textbook ahead of time. In class, discuss the textbook, questions, and sample assignments. You may want to work on parts of your assignment in class. Be sure to share discoveries made in the previous week's assignment.

c. Develop your own lesson plans and use the textbook as a supplement to be read by your students. Be sure to use the assignments in the textbook. No one can learn how to study the Bible without doing actual studies. This course will never work with a lecture-only approach.

4. How much time you take for prayer in your group will depend on your group's needs and available time. It is imperative, however, that you allow plenty of time for the study.

5. As you teach, be sure to use illustrations of all the techniques you introduce. That is the purpose for the sample assignments at the end of most chapters. Principles are much more difficult to follow than examples.

6. Encourage your students each week. This course is hard work, and students need your uplifting help to keep them going at times. The following suggestions will help you with this:

a. Do all the assignments yourself. Class members feel much better if you are working alongside them.

b. Remind them to do what they can and not worry about those parts of an assignment that seem to be beyond their reach. Be realistic with them and encourage them to do the same with themselves. *Remember* that completing the lessons is not half as important as learning how to study and opening the door for God to change their lives.

c. Do not let them compare each other's progress. If you have a star pupil who likes to show off her scholastic abilities or spiritual insights, try to help her see that such action only hurts other class members. Never let any student hog the sharing time.

d. Encourage every member to share something. Never belittle or argue with a student who may not have done the assignment just right or whose answer was off the track. If something comes up that needs correction, go to the person in private. Ask the Lord to give you wisdom and tact so as not to crush spirits.

e. Answer all questions directed toward you. If you do not have an answer, say so, and plan ways to find it before the next meeting. Never make any student feel foolish because of the nature of a question.

f. Remind students regularly of the tremendous benefits of this kind of study.

g. Ask God for the gift of encouragement!

7. It will be helpful to have on hand, at your class sessions, the following tools for reference, particularly if you are doing any assignment work in class:

　a. Bible dictionary

　b. Bible atlas

　c. Concordance

8. Here is a list of other books that may enrich your background as you prepare to teach your class:

Eerdman's Handbook of the Bible, by David and Pat Alexander. Eerdman's Publishing Company, 1973.

Exploring the Scriptures, by John Phillips. Moody Press, 1965.

How to Study the Bible, edited by John B. Job. Inter-Varsity Press, 1973.

Knowing Scripture, by R. C. Sproul. Inter-Varsity Press, 1977.

Let's Study the Bible, by Kenneth E. Jones. Warner Press, 1962.

The Literature of the Bible, by Leland Ryken. Zondervan Publishing House, 1974.

Understanding the Bible, by John R. W. Stott. Zondervan Publishing House, 1979.

Why Believe the Bible, by John MacArthur. Regal Books, 1980.

The Zondervan Pictorial Encyclopedia of the Bible, edited by Merrill C. Tenney. Zondervan Publishing House, 1975.

Teaching this class can be one of the highlights of your Christian experience. Pray daily that the Lord will guide you into a true adventure of sharing the yoke with Him in the lives of the students He gathers around you for study.

APPENDIX 2

Plan 1   BIBLE OVERVIEW READING PLAN

Read the following books in the order given:

Genesis	Isaiah
Exodus	Luke
Joshua	Matthew
Judges	Acts
Ruth	Romans
1, 2 Samuel	Hebrews
1, 2 Kings	Ephesians
Psalms	Colossians
Ecclesiiastes	1, 2 Corinthians
Proverbs	Galatians
Ezra	1, 2 Peter
Nehemiah	1, 2 Timothy
Amos	James
Hosea	1, 2, 3 John
	Revelation

Plan 2   READ-IT-THROUGH-IN-A-YEAR PLANS

1. Read 3 chapters a day, 5 on Sunday—In this way, you will read through Old and New Testaments once.

2. Read 4 chapters a day, 6 on Sunday—In this way, you will read the Old Testament once and the New twice.

3. Write to one of the following organizations for a daily reading schedule:

American Bible Society
P.O. Box 5677
Grand Central Station
New York, NY 10163

Back to the Bible Broadcast
Box 82808
Lincoln, NE 68501

National Association of Evangelicals
Box 28
Wheaton, IL 60187

Plan 3   SELECTED READINGS

Order reading schedules from the following:
American Bible Society (see address above)

Scripture Union
1716 Spruce Street
Philadelphia, PA 19103

Plan 4   OTHER SOURCES OF READING PLANS

How to Study the Bible for Yourself, by Tim LaHaye. Harvest House, 1976.

Halley's Bible Handbook, by Henry Halley. Zondervan Publishing House, 1968.

Why Believe the Bible, by John MacArthur. Regal Books, 1980.

APPENDIX 3

FINDING WORD MEANINGS
IN YOUR CONCORDANCE

Strong's Exhaustive Concordance of the Bible not only has a complete concordance, in which you can find every reference to every word that is used in the Bible. It also has two original language dictionaries in the back of the book. First comes the Hebrew and Chaldee dictionary, with word entries numbering from 1 through 8674. After that comes a Greek dictionary with word entries numbering from 1 through 5624.

The definitions in those dictionaries contain a number of complicated symbols and abbreviations that you will not fully understand. There is a key to those in the introduction to the Hebrew dictionary. Consult the key if you have questions. For most purposes, you will not need to pursue them in detail. Generally, you will see notes such as *lit.*, meaning literal, *fig.*, meaning figurative, and *prim. root,* meaning primary root. Beyond those, you can pretty much leave the rest to the pros.

Most editions of this concordance are in the King James version of the Bible. However, it is now available in some of the modern translations as well. There is even an edition that has a comparative section covering six different versions.

How do you use this tool? Let us suppose you want to look for the meaning of the word *deliverance.*

First, look for the word *deliverance* in the concordance sec-

deliverance See also DELIVERANCES.
Ge 45: 7 save your lives by a great *d'*.   **6413**
J'g 15:18 Thou hast given this great *d'*   **8668**
2Ki 5: 1 Lord had given *d'* unto Syria: * "
    13:17 The arrow of the Lord's *d',*   * "
       17 the arrow of *d'* from Syria   * "
1Ch 11:14 Lord saved them by a great *d'*.   * "
2Ch 12: 7 but I will grant them some *d';*   **6413**
Ez   9:13 hast given us such *d'* as this;   * "
Es   4:14 enlargement and *d'* arise to the   **2020**
Ps 18:50 Great *d'* giveth he to his king;   **3444**
    32: 7 me about with the songs of *d'*.   **6405**
Isa 26:18 we have not wrought any *d'* in   **3444**
Joel 2:32 and in Jerusalem shall be *d'*   *6413
Ob   17 upon Mount Zion shall be *d'*   * "
Lu   4:18 to preach *d'* to the captives, and   *859
Heb 11:35 were tortured, not accepting *d';*   829

Figure 2

tion of the book. Here (see fig. 2),[1] you find a list of all the instances where the word is used in the Bible. Along with each reference, you will find, in the right-hand column, another number. Those numbers refer to the word meaning entries in the dictionaries. Numbers in bold print refer to the Hebrew dictionary; numbers in italics refer to the Greek dictionary.

In our sample, there are five bold numbers and two italicized ones. So we will suppose that we want to find the meaning of the word that is used in Genesis 45:7. The number for that word is 6413.

Having the number, you look it up in the Hebrew and Chaldee dictionary (see fig. 3).[2] Note several things in this definition. First is the Hebrew word (in fact, here there are two of them) written in both Hebrew letters and English, for pronunciation. Next, it tells us that this is the feminine form of the word 6412; that its meaning is "deliverance"; that it is, in concrete words, "an escaped portion." Finally, there is a list of all the other words that are used in the King James Bible to translate this same Hebrew word.

Because it refers us to 6412, we go there and find that it means "a refugee," and comes from 6403. Checking back at 6403, we discover a primary root word, meaning "to spit out, escape, deliver."

1. From James Strong, *Strong's Exhaustive Concordance of the Bible* (Nashville: Abingdon-Cokesbury, 1980), p. 253.
2. Ibid., p. 95.

6403. פָּלַט **pâlaṭ**, *paw-lat'*; a prim. root; to *slip* out, i.e. *escape*; causat. to *deliver:*— calve, carry away safe, deliver, (cause to) escape.

6404. פֶּלֶט **Peleṭ**, *peh'-let*; from 6403; *escape*; *Pelet*, the name of two Isr.:—Pelet. See also 1046.

פָּלֵט **pâlêṭ**. See 6412.

6405. פַּלֵּט **pallêṭ**, *pal-late'*; from 6403; *escape:*— deliverance, escape.

פְּלֵטָה **pelêṭâh**. See 6413.

6406. פַּלְטִי **Palṭîy**, *pal-tee'*; from 6403; *delivered*; *Palti*, the name of two Isr.:—Palti, Phalti.

6407. פַּלְטִי **Palṭîy**, *pal-tee'*; patron. from 6406; a *Paltite* or desc. of Palti:—Paltite.

6408. פִּלְטַי **Pilṭay**, *pil-tah'ee*; for 6407; *Piltai*, an Isr.:—Piltai.

6409. פַּלְטִיאֵל **Palṭîy'êl**, *pal-tee-ale'*; from the same as 6404 and 410; *deliverance of God*; *Paltiël*, the name of two Isr.:—Paltiel, Phaltiel.

6410. פְּלַטְיָה **Pelaṭyâh**, *pel-at-yaw'*; or

פְּלַטְיָהוּ **Pelaṭyâhûw**, *pel-at-yaw'-hoo*; from 6403 and 3050; *Jah has delivered*; *Pelatjah*, the name of four Isr.:—Pelatiah.

פָּלִיא **pâlîy'**. See 6383.

6411. פְּלָיָה **Pelâyâh**, *pel-aw-yaw'*; or

פְּלָאיָה **Pelá'yâh**, *pel-aw-yaw'*; from 6381 and 3050; *Jah has distinguished*; *Pelaiah*, the name of three Isr.:—Pelaiah.

6412. פָּלִיט **pâlîyṭ**, *paw-leet'*; or

פָּלֵיט **pâlêyṭ**, *paw-late'*; or

פָּלֵט **pâlêṭ**, *paw-late'*; from 6403; a *refugee:*—(that have) escape (-d, -th), fugitive.

6413. פְּלֵיטָה **pelêyṭâh**, *pel-ay-taw'*; or

פְּלֵטָה **pelêṭâh**, *pel-ay-taw'*; fem. of 6412; *deliverance*; concr. an *escaped portion:*—deliverance. (that is) escape (-d), remnant.

Figure 3

To check further into the meanings, you might want to look for reference to the other words—*escape* and *remnant*. Also follow the same process with the Greek word, *859* (see fig. 4).[3] Here we find an expanded meaning to include freedom, pardon, liberty, forgiveness, remission.

3. Ibid., p. 17.

855. ἄφεσις **aphĕsis**, *af'-es-is;* from *863; freedom;* (fig.) *pardon:*—deliverance, forgiveness, liberty, remission.

800. ἀφή **haphē**, *haf-ay';* from *680;* prob. a *ligament (as fastening):*—joint.

861. ἀφθαρσία **aphtharsia**, *af-thar-see'-ah;* from *862; incorruptibility;* gen. *unending existence;* (fig.) *genuineness:*—immortality, incorruption, sincerity.

862. ἄφθαρτος **aphthartŏs**, *af'-thar-tos;* from *r* (as a neg. particle) and a der. of *5351; undecaying* (in essence or continuance):—not (in-, un-) corruptible, immortal.

863. ἀφίημι **aphiēmi**, *af-ee'-ay-mee;* from *575* and ἵημι **hiemi** (to *send;* an intens. form of εἶμι **ĕimi**, to *go*); to *send forth,* in various applications (as follow):—cry, forgive, forsake, lay aside, leave, let (alone, be, go, have), omit, put (send) away, remit, suffer, yield up.

Figure 4

If you use *Young's Analytical Concordance,* you will need to follow a different procedure. Directions are given clearly in the introductory pages, and it is easy to understand.

APPENDIX 4

Here is a list of other books that may be helpful to you as you learn how to study your Bible. Again, as in the tools list in lesson 3, they are marked according to understanding level (S=simple; D=deep; H=heavy).

S *Autobiography of God*, by Lloyd John Ogilvie. Regal Books, 1979.

S *Daring to Draw Near*, by John White. Inter-Varsity Press, 1977.

H *Interpreting the Bible*, by J. Stafford Wright. Inter-Varsity Press, 1955.

D *Knowing Scripture*, by R. C. Sproul. Inter-Varsity Press, 1977.

H *Literature of the Bible*, by Leland Ryken. Zondervan Publishing House, 1974.

D *Understanding the Bible*, by John R. W. Stott. Zondervan Publishing House, 1979.